Glacier and Waterton Lakes National Parks

Glacier National Park: The Basics

History and Facts

Established: May 11, 1910

Visitors: Glacier 3,000,000 / Waterton Lakes 500,000

Designations: Waterton-Glacier International Peace Park; World Heritage Site; Biosphere Reserve; International Dark Sky Park

National Historic Landmarks: Going-to-the-Sun Road, Lake McDonald Lodge, Many Glacier Hotel, Granite Park Chalet, Sperry Chalet, Two Medicine Store

National Scenic Trails: Continental Divide National Scenic Trail in the United States and the Great Divide Trail in Canada

States/provinces: Montana and Alberta

Time zone: Mountain Time Zone

Official park websites: nps.gov/glacier and pc.gc.ca/en/pn-np/ab/waterton/

Physical Features

Acreage: Glacier is 1,013,572.42 acres (4,104.97 square kilometers); Waterton is roughly 124,788 acres (505 square kilometers).

Elevation: Glacier's lowest point 3,150' (960 m) at junction of Middle and North Forks of Flathead River; highest point, Mount Cleveland, at 10,466' (3,192 m); Waterton's lowest point, 4,200' (1,280 m) at the townsite; highest point, Mount Blakiston, 9,645' (2,940 m).

Geologic features: Glacier—Triple Divide, where the water flows to three drainages: west to the Pacific Ocean, southeast to the Gulf of Mexico, and east/northeast to Hudson Bay; 26 active glaciers; Lewis Thrust, where the rock layers pushed up and folded, runs from Marias Pass through Waterton; at 487' (148 m), Upper Waterton Lake is deepest lake within Canadian Rockies; evidence of the Belt Sea is found on much of the sedimentary rocks within both parks.

Water resources: In Glacier, 762 lakes, 563 streams, 4 rivers. Waterton has 1 river, approximately 80 lakes; over 100 km of streams; over 200 waterfalls between both parks.

Annual precipitation: West Glacier, 29" (74 cm) rain and 157" (399 cm) snowfall; St. Mary, 27" (69 cm), 120" (305 cm) snowfall; Waterton townsite, 42" (107 cm) rain, 225" (575 cm) snowfall.

Wind: The east sides of Glacier and Waterton Lakes are known for their high winds with an average daily velocity of 18 mph (30 km/h), with gusts over 60 mph (100 km/h).

Temperature range: 100 degrees F (38 C) to -56 F (-49 C); average temperature in West Glacier in July, 80 degrees F (26 C); in January, 30 degrees F (-1 C); average temperature in Waterton in July, 73 degrees F (23 C); in January, 31 degrees F (-1 C).

Plant species: 1,132 vascular plants, including 127 non-native species; over 850 mosses, lichens, and fungi species.

Animal species: Over 20 fish species; 71 mammal species; 276 bird species; 71 reptile species; 6 amphibian species; over 50 butterfly species.

Wildlife population estimates: 1,200–2,500 mountain goats; bighorn sheep, 450–600; black bears, 600–700; wolves, 8 packs (roughly 35 animals); 1,040 grizzlies in Northern Continental Divide Ecosystem.

Facilities

Entrance stations: Glacier, 5: Polebridge (mid-May to end of September); West Glacier (open all year); Two Medicine; St. Mary; Many Glacier (mid-May to early October); . Waterton Lakes, 1 (open all year).

Roads: Glacier's Going-to-the-Sun Road, 50 miles (80 km) (end of June to mid-October to vehicles); paved. Waterton's Akamina and Red Rock Parkways are each 9–10 miles (14–16 km) one-way, paved.

Trails: Glacier, 745 miles (1,199 km); Waterton, 120 miles (200 km); approximately 65 trailheads in Glacier and 30 in Waterton Lakes.

Campgrounds: Glacier, 65 backcountry sites; Waterton Lakes, 9 backcountry sites; Glacier, 13 frontcountry campgrounds with 1,004 sites; Waterton Lakes, 3 frontcountry campgrounds with over 300 sites.

Picnic areas: Glacier, 8; Waterton, 8.

Fuel: Glacier: West Glacier, East Glacier, St. Mary, and Babb. Waterton: Pat's Waterton in the townsite (spring through fall), otherwise either Mountain View, Cardston or Pincher Creek, AB.

Medical services: Glacier: West Glacier, Kalispell, Whitefish, Browning. Waterton: Pincher Creek, Cardston, or Blairmore, AB.

Nature Guide to Glacier and Waterton Lakes National Parks

Amy Grisak

FALCON GUIDES

GUILFORD, CONNECTICUT

An imprint of The Rowman & Littlefield Publishing Group, Inc.
4501 Forbes Blvd., Ste. 200
Lanham, MD 20706
www.rowman.com

Falcon and FalconGuides are registered trademarks and Make Adventure Your Story is a trademark of The Rowman & Littlefield Publishing Group, Inc.

Distributed by NATIONAL BOOK NETWORK

Copyright © 2021 The Rowman & Littlefield Publishing Group, Inc.

Map by The Rowman & Littlefield Publishing Group, Inc.

Photos by Amy Grisak except where otherwise indicated

British Library Cataloguing in Publication Information available

Library of Congress Cataloging-in-Publication Data available

ISBN 978-1-4930-4467-2 (paper: alk. paper)
ISBN 978-1-4930-4468-9 (electronic)

∞™ The paper used in this publication meets the minimum requirements of American National Standard for Information Sciences—Permanence of Paper for Printed Library Materials, ANSI/NISO Z39.48-1992.

Contents

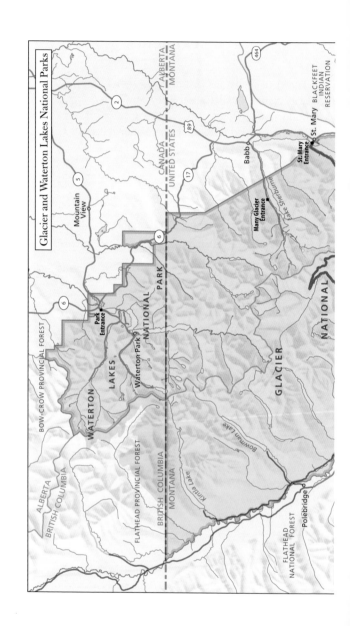

Glacier and Waterton Lakes National Parks

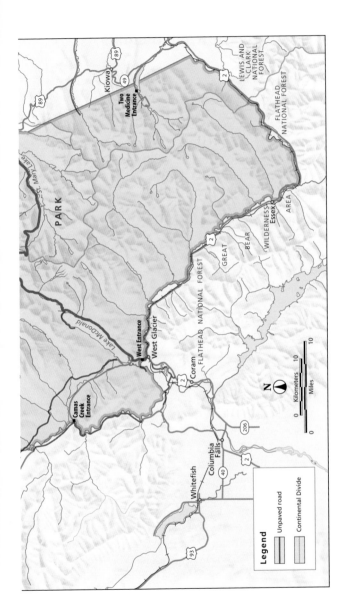

Acknowledgments

Recognizing everyone who flamed my love of Glacier and Waterton Lakes and expanded my knowledge of the region over the past thirty years would take the entirety of this book, but there are a number of individuals who walked hand in hand with me during this most recent journey.

First and foremost, a huge thanks to our sons, Samuel and John, who traipsed throughout the hills and forests with me in search of the flowers, birds, and wildlife we needed to photograph in order show others. Thanks to my scientist husband, Grant, for critiquing the sections multiple times, and joining us in search of pika, fish, and mushrooms.

I would like to thank Lauren Alley, Chris Downs, Mark Biel, John Waller, Anya Tyson, Jessi Mejia, Jami Belt, Lisa Bates, Tara Carolin, and all of the amazing Glacier National Park staff. My heartfelt gratitude goes out to Dallas Meidinger, Barb Johnston, Genoa Alger, Edwin Knox, Sarah Davidson, Paul Harper, Helena Mahoney, Caitlin Willier, and Rob Sissons at Waterton Lakes National Park, who answered questions and reviewed content throughout the process. Thank you to John Ashley, for pointing out Glacier's finest, as well as the amazing harlequin ducks; to Mark Schnee for his stonefly lesson; and to Doug Mitchell, John Donovan, and the wonderful crew at the Glacier National Park Conservancy for their hard work in supporting this precious resource.

Thanks to Richard Krott of Tizer Botanical Gardens and Arboretum, who is quick to point out the nuances among the trees; to my longtime friend Brenda Griswold, who is just as excited about pixie cup lichen as I am (and maybe leery of trail cameras) and accompanied us on some of our adventures, along with the sharp-eyed Vicky Tronstad; to our local Great Falls Nature Club kids, who are champion frog finders; to Tim Wheeler for opening my eyes to the often-overlooked fungal world; and to Tanya Murphy and her enthusiasm for the 5-needle pines.

I would be remiss if I didn't express my appreciation to Evan Helminger, the editor at FalconGuides who first asked if I was interested in chatting about potential book projects and guided me through the steps of launching this project. I am equally grateful to be in the highly capable hands of Mason Gadd, Emily Chiarelli, and Melissa Hayes, as well as all of the phenomenal staff at FalconGuides, who are focused on creating an exceptional resource for our readers. Most of all, I want to thank the visitors of Glacier and Waterton Lakes National Parks who love these national treasures as much as I do. Their care is what will preserve these special places for our children and grandchildren so they will be able to listen to the loons call on St. Mary Lake or watch grizzlies graze along a distant slope just like we can today.

Glacier National Park Conservancy

As the nonprofit arm of our beloved Glacier National Park, the Glacier National Park Conservancy funds many, if not most, of the projects necessary for public safety and the preservation of park features, along with myriad opportunities to provide a deeper experience for visitors and research projects needed to answer questions about the wildlife and ecosystems. From providing the hiker/biker shuttles in the spring, presenting the Native America Speaks events, creating accessible trails for visitors with mobility issues, or housing a world-class telescope in the new observatory for the astronomy program, the GNPC focuses on bringing out the best of the park. In short, they are the reason we have nice things.

Since science is the backbone of the park, the GNPC supports the Citizen Scientist program, along with in-depth research to better understand everything from threatened alpine stoneflies to lynx populations. This research translates into school programs and field trips, including distance learning and professional development for educators to pass this information on to the next generation.

But they cannot do it by themselves. With well over three million visitors to Glacier each season, the list of needs and projects to make their experience better never ends. For those who love the park, it benefits everyone to support them as a Friend of the Glacier National Park Conservancy to help further their efforts. To see their long list of endeavors, shop their store, or become a Friend of Glacier, visit them at glacier.org or call (406) 892-3250.

Introduction

After decades of interacting with park visitors and years of leading friends and their kids on the trails, I have found that people have the same questions about flowers, wildlife, birds, and the parks' remarkable geology. In this compact, colorful book you will discover the most common species, along with a few rarely seen residents, such as wolverines, which might be a once-in-a-lifetime experience. The scientific names and families are included, but more-vivid details on the life cycles and unique characteristics of each will create a memorable picture. For those who wish to delve more deeply into the scientific specifics, take a look at the "References" section at the end of this book for a list of excellent resources.

A better understanding of these individual plants and animals inspires all of us to preserve and protect everything from the tiniest butterfly to the magnificent grizzly. With close to four million people visiting Glacier and Waterton Lakes National Parks every year, the future of the parks rests firmly upon our shoulders. Every action has a ripple effect. If just half the annual visitors picked a flower, nearly two million blossoms would be gone every season. If we want our next visit, or our grandchildren's visits decades down the road, to be the same awe-inspiring experience, we must take responsibility for this precious resource that belongs to all of us. Take photos of the flowers, but please don't pick them. Give wildlife a wide berth. Be kind to the landscape. Our trails are some of the best in the world, but when we make our own, it degrades the entire system. Most of all, breathe in the beauty of this stunning environment so it never leaves your heart.

About Glacier and Waterton Lakes National Parks

Breathtaking mountain scenery with glaciers and snowfields lingering in the high country throughout the summer, lush valleys, and ample water make Glacier and Waterton Lakes a recreationist's paradise. This wonder wasn't lost on Glacier's early advocates, including the eminent conservationist George Bird Grinnell, who is honored with a glacier, lake, and a mountain named for him. He finally saw the creation of the park on May 11, 1910. Billed as the "See America First" campaign, courtesy of the Great Northern Railway, wealthy Easterners had the chance to experience the magnificent Western landscape, boasting scenery rivaling the European Alps, with luxurious accommodations to match.

The inception of Waterton Lakes initially took a different route. Before 1900, the Canadian government preserved Waterton as a Dominion Forest Park, yet its natural wealth was more

Piegan Glacier from Preston Park

fully realized when Glacier and Waterton Lakes joined in 1932, as Rotarians on both sides of the border pushed to create the world's first international peace park. Bordering northwestern Montana and southern Alberta, there's a striking difference in appearance on the west and east sides of Glacier, along with Waterton Lakes. Rain is more generous on the west side, resulting in enormous trees, dense forests, and vegetation indicative of this moister region. The east side is harsher, with drier conditions and far more wind, but it boasts stunning scenery as mountains overlap in the landscape. Waterton Lakes offers the best of both worlds: It has more rain and snow than the prairie, yet it's situated where the mountains meet the prairie, providing equally stunning views any time of the year.

The visitor centers / centre are the best places to obtain information on trails, parking lots, area closures, and weather conditions. Most are open from mid-May to mid-September, although Apgar is sometimes open on the weekends beyond those months, and the Waterton Visitor Centre is open year-round. Also check the campground kiosks and ranger stations for information on ranger-led hikes and interpretive talks.

The Logan Pass Visitor Center

Glacier's convenient dashboard feature, the Glacier Information Display at nps.gov/applications/glac/dashboard/, provides up-to-date information on the status of roads and weather. Waterton Lakes National Park posts updates and closures, as well as general visitor information, on their website: pc.gc.ca/en/pn-np/ab/waterton/.

There is a misconception that Glacier is closed during the winter. Going-to-the-Sun Road closes for vehicle traffic by the third week of October, and restaurants and other facilities are shut down for the season, but cross-country skiing and snowshoeing along Lake McDonald or the Camas Road are increasingly popular. Many people also love heading to the more-remote Autumn Creek Trail located near Marias Pass. Like Glacier, Waterton Lakes is much quieter in the winter, but still provides a memorable opportunity for cross-country skiers and snowshoers to explore the frozen landscape in peace. Some accommodations remain open in Waterton Lakes, but it is far from busy.

When the plow crews start clearing Going-to-the-Sun Road in the spring, it is open to bicyclists and hikers months before vehicles crowd the thoroughfare, and Waterton has several roads open only to hikers and bikers early in the season.

It's not until July, and sometimes toward the end of that month, that trails such as Grinnell Glacier or the Carthew-Alderson Trail are sufficiently cleared of snow to allow safe passage for the average hiker.

Lodging is a hot commodity during this peak season, and reservations at lodges and some campgrounds need to be made months, if not a year, ahead of time. Advanced reservations for some sites in Apgar, Fish Creek, St. Mary, and Many Glacier can be requested at nps.gov/glac/planyourvisit/camping.htm. For the Waterton Lakes townsite campgrounds, call (877) 737-3783 or visit pc.gc.ca/en/pn-np/ab/waterton/activ/camping/camping-reservation. For hotel or cabin reservations, contact Xanterra, (855) 733-4522; glaciernationalparklodges.com/lodging; or Pursuit Glacier Park Collection, (844) 868-7474, glacierparkcollection.com. Granite Park and Sperry Chalet reservations open once a year, typically in January. To apply, or to check availability status, call (888) 345-2649, or visit graniteparkchalet.com or sperry chalet.com.

Both parks turn visitors away at the gate in certain areas when the parking reaches capacity. People with reservations are permitted to proceed, but even so, finding a parking space can be daunting. To avoid this situation, stay in the area the night before if you're planning a hike, or arrive very early, and always have a backup plan.

There are separate entrance fees to visit Glacier and Waterton Lakes National Parks. For Glacier, visitors purchase a single-day, weekly, motorcycle-entry, annual pass for Glacier, or annual pass for the entire National Park system, either at the gate or digitally through yourpassnow.com. These are available on digital devices, although keep in mind that not all entrance stations have cell or Wi-Fi availability. The Every Kid in a Park program provides a free annual National Park pass to all fourth graders who apply online at everykidinapark.org.

Waterton Lakes offers either daily or annual Discovery park passes, and all persons under seventeen years old are admitted for free. To purchase the Discovery pass online, go to pc.gc.ca/en/voyage-travel/admission.

Even though Glacier and Waterton Lakes make up an international peace park, visitors still need a passport to cross the border going either direction. There are customs border stations along the Chief Mountain Road, as well as the Port of Piegan / Carway on US 89 and AB 2, as well as the Goat Haunt Ranger Station at the southern end of Waterton Lake. Reporting Offsite Arrival Mobile (ROAM) kiosks in Waterton Lakes townsite allow hikers and backpackers to report in or out when traveling. Visit CBP.gov for more information.

Common Destinations in or around Glacier and Waterton Lakes

The west side of Glacier is bustling by early May, particularly on the weekends, due to the fact that people can hike or bicycle

Cars driving through the tunnel along Going-to-the-Sun Road

Going-to-the-Sun Road while it is still closed to vehicle traffic. Avalanche Campground is used for additional parking during the spring season to handle the massive amount of bicyclists, yet be aware that it is still difficult to find a parking spot on the weekends. Another option is to take the free hiker/biker shuttle from Lake McDonald Lodge. Visitors also travel the Camas Road and head to Polebridge.

During the summer, Going-to-the-Sun Road is a must-see. As a result, it's often bumper-to-bumper traffic, with people vying for the limited parking spots along the way. Logan Pass Visitor Center—the midway point, and a favorite hiking trailhead—is typically filled by eight a.m. Besides restrooms at the Apgar, Logan Pass, and St. Mary Visitor Centers, there are facilities along the Going-to-the-Sun Road, including Lake McDonald Lodge, Avalanche picnic area, the Loop, the parking area east of Jackson Glacier Lookout, Sun Point picnic area, and Rising Sun.

Many Glacier is one of the most beautiful regions within Glacier, and even though it is not part of the Going-to-the-Sun corridor, it is so popular that rangers sometimes limit the number of vehicles that can enter. The Many Glacier Road is found 9 miles north of St. Mary near the town of Babb.

Polebridge and the North Fork are equally popular in Glacier. The North Fork Road is notoriously bumpy and dusty, but as long as you drive slowly, it is fine for most vehicles (4WDs are not necessary in the summer). Bowman and Kintla Lakes are beautiful, tree-surrounded wilderness lakes, but visitor use is limited during the summer. Go early if you want to make it there to hear the loons.

In Waterton Lakes, besides the multiple hiking opportunities, driving the Akamina and Red Rock Parkways is a favorite means of catching a glimpse of wildlife. Fuel and food are easily found in town, and the newly renovated (after the 2017 Kenow Wildfire) Crandall Mountain Campground is a local favorite.

Services in and around Glacier and Waterton Lakes

Gas Stations
West Glacier: West Glacier Gas Station, (406) 888-5558; Glacier Highland, open year-round, (406) 888-5427
East Glacier: Bear Track Travel Center, open year-round, (406) 226-5504
St. Mary: St. Mary's RB; Exxon
Babb: Thronson's General Store, (406) 732-5530

Repair and Towing
Columbia Falls Auto Clinic (repairs), (406) 892-2220
Loren's Auto Repair, (406) 755-7757
OH's Towing (Columbia Falls), (406) 892-1600
Advanced Automotive, Tires, and Towing (Browning), (406) 338-4445

Lodging
Xanterra, (855) 733-4522; glaciernationalparklodges.com/lodging
Village Inn at Apgar: south shore of Lake McDonald

Lake McDonald Lodge: at the northeastern end of Lake McDonald

Rising Sun Motor Inn & Cabins: 6 miles west of the St. Mary Visitor Center

Many Glacier Hotel: on the northeast shore of Swiftcurrent Lake

Swiftcurrent Motor Inn & Cabins: at the end of Many Glacier Road

Pursuit Glacier Park Collection, (844) 868-7474; glacier parkcollection.com

Belton Chalet: south side of US 2 just outside of West Glacier

West Glacier RV Park and Cabins: located behind West Glacier

West Glacier Village: east and outside of the West Entrance

Apgar Village Lodge & Cabins: south shore of Lake McDonald

Glacier Park Lodge: near East Glacier townsite

St. Mary Village: a mile east of the St. Mary entrance

Prince of Wales: overlooking Upper Waterton Lake

Izaak Walton Inn, (406) 888-5700; izaakwaltoninn.com

Izaak Walton Inn: midway between West and East Glacier on US 2

Summit Mountain Lodge, (406) 226-9319; summitmtn lodge.com

Summit Mountain Lodge: near Marias Pass on southern edge of Glacier

Waterton Glacier Suites, (403) 859-2004; watertonsuites .com

Waterton Glacier Suites: in the Waterton townsite

Bayshore Inn Resort & Spa, (403) 859-2211; bayshoreinn .com

Bayshore Inn Resort & Spa: near the west shore of Upper Waterton Lake

Waterton Lakes Lodge Resort, (403) 859-2150; waterton lakeslodge.com

Waterton Lakes Lodge: in the Waterton townsite

Crandell Mountain Lodge, (403) 859-2288; crandellmoun
tainlodge.com

Crandell Mountain Lodge: north end of the Waterton
townsite

Aspen Village, (403) 859-2255; aspenvillageinn.com

Aspen Village: in the Waterton townsite

Camping

Advanced reservations available for Fish Creek, St. Mary, Many
Glacier, or group reservations for Apgar through recreation.gov.
Other campgrounds are first come, first serve:

Kintla Lake: 13 sites (no vehicles/trailers over 21' [6 m],
tents only)

Bowman Lake: 46 sites (no vehicles/trailers over 21' [6 m])

Logging Creek: 7 sites (tents only)

Fish Creek: 179 sites (no utility hookups, shower in loop A)

Apgar: 194 sites (no utility hookups, 23 sites fit a truck/
camper or RV that is 40' [12 m] long, near grocery and
restaurants)

Sprague Creek: 25 sites (no towed units, grocery and restaurant nearby)

Avalanche Campground: 87 sites (shuttle stop)

Rising Sun: 84 sites (camp store, restaurant, and pay showers nearby)

St. Mary: 148 sites (showers, dishwashing station, close to
restaurants, shops)

Many Glacier: 109 sites (restaurant, gift shop, pay showers
at Swiftcurrent Motor Inn)

Cutbank: 14 sites (no potable water available)

Two Medicine: 100 sites (potable water, dishwashing station, camp store nearby)

Waterton Townsite Campground: 237 sites (some full hookups, Wi-Fi, hot water in wash houses)

Belly River: 24 sites (tent only, no potable water)

Crandell Mountain: 129 sites (winter camping facilities, flush toilets)

Visitor Centers / Rangers Stations

For all Glacier visitor questions, call (406) 888-7800.

Apgar Visitor Center: Apgar, mid-May to mid-October

Apgar Backcountry Office: Apgar, early May to end of October; off-season, (406) 888-7800

Apgar Nature Center: Apgar, mid-June to end of August

Travel Alberta West Glacier Information Centre: West Glacier, (406) 888-5743

Park Headquarters: 64 Grinnell Drive, West Glacier, (406) 888-7800; open Monday–Friday

Walton Ranger Station: Essex, beginning of June to end of August

Polebridge Ranger Station: North Fork, end of May to end of September

Logan Pass: Logan Pass, end of June to first part of September

St. Mary Visitor Center: St. Mary entrance, end of May to October

St. Mary Backcountry Office in St. Mary Visitor Center: end of May to end of September

Many Glacier Ranger Station: Many Glacier, end of May to end of September

Two Medicine Ranger Station: Two Medicine, June 1 to end of September

Waterton Lakes National Park Visitor Centre: Waterton townsite, (403) 859-5133

Boat Docks, Boat Tours, and Trail Rides

Boat tours: Glacier Park Boat Company, glacierparkboats.com

Boat tours tend to fill up quickly during the peak seasons. Reserve a spot months in advance on their website.

Lake McDonald: boat tours; boat rentals

St. Mary Lake: boat tours; boat rentals
Two Medicine Lake: boat tours; boat rentals
Many Glacier: boat tours; boat rentals
Waterton Lakes; Waterton Shoreline Cruise Company,
 (403) 859-2362; watertoncruise.com

Other equipment rentals: For kayak, paddleboard, bike, fishing equipment, camping gear, and bear spray rentals, visit Glacier Outfitters in Apgar, (406) 219-7466; goglacieroutfitters.com.

For those who bring their own watercraft, it's required to have your boat inspected prior to using the waters in either park, or in state or provincial check stations in the East, Midwest, and South. Invasive zebra and quagga mussels are fingernail-size mollusks that severely impact water quality. They are transported from one water body to another by attaching themselves to watercraft. Once established, they cling in groups to anything in the water, as well as spoiling beaches with their sharp, smelly shells. The mussels filter a liter of water a day, eliminating the plankton and nutrients fish and other species depend upon, completely disrupting the ecosystem. To protect this precious resource, regulations are enforced, including sealing trailered motorized boats to their trailers for a specific amount of time and inspections for human-powered watercraft.

Horseback rides: The sole concessionaire within Glacier National Park is Swan Mountain Outfitters, with corrals in Apgar, along the east side of Lake McDonald, as well as in the parking area above the Many Glacier Hotel: (406) 387-4405; swanmountainglacier .com.

In Waterton, the Alpine Stables offers one-hour to all-day rides, including to the Alderson-Carthew Summit: (403) 859-2462; alpinestables.com.

Restaurants, Cafes, and Snack Shops
Polebridge: Polebridge Mercantile, Northern Lights Saloon

West Glacier: Belton Grill Dining Room & Tap Room, Highland Cafe, West Glacier Restaurant, Glacier Coffee House, Freda's Bar

Apgar: Eddie's Cafe & Mercantile

Lake McDonald Lodge: Jammer Joe's Grill & Pizzeria, Lucke's Lounge, Russell's Fireside Dining Room, camp store

Rising Sun: Two Dog Flats Grill, camp store

St. Mary: Snowgoose Grille, Glacier Perk Espresso Shop, Johnson's of St. Mary Restaurant, Two Sisters Cafe, Rising Sun Pizza, Frogs Cantina, Kip's Beer Garden

Many Glacier: Ptarmigan Dining Room, Swiss Lounge, Heidi's Snack Shop & Espresso Stand, Nell's at Swiftcurrent Restaurant, camp store at Swiftcurrent, Cattle Baron Supper Club

East Glacier: Great Northern Dining Room, Empire Lounge, Empire Cafe, Country Corner, Rock 'n Roll Bakery, Two Medicine Grill, Summit Mountain Lodge & Steakhouse

Waterton: Royal Stewart Dining Room, Windsor Lounge, Windflower Avenue Corner Coffee, Pearl's Cafe, Thirsty Bear Kitchen & Bar, Wieners of Waterton, The Lakeside Chophouse at Bayshore, Pizza of Waterton, Vimy's Lounge & Grill, Trappers Mountain Grill, Big Scoop Ice Cream Parlour

Groceries, Supplies, and Gifts

Polebridge: Polebridge Mercantile

West Glacier: West Glacier T-Shirt Shop, West Glacier Mercantile, Glacier Natural History Association, Glacier Highland convenience store, West Glacier gas station and supplies

Apgar: Eddie's Cafe & Mercantile, Montana House gift shop, Cedar Tree gift shop, Schoolhouse Gifts

Lake McDonald Lodge: general store and gift store

Rising Sun: camp store

St. Mary: Snowgoose gift shop, Park Cafe & Grocery, St. Mary Grocery, Trail & Creek Outfitters Gift Shop, camp store at St. Mary KOA

Many Glacier: Hotel gift shop, camp store at Swiftcurrent Motor Inn

Waterton: Rocky Mountain Foodmart, Caribou Clothes, The Tamarack, The Village Gift Shop, Trappers Trading Post, Evergreen Gifts, Zum's Mercantile & Bear Shop

Showers and Laundry

St. Mary: Johnson's of St. Mary, laundry and showers; St. Mary KOA, laundry

Many Glacier: Swiftcurrent Motor Inn & Cabins, laundry and showers

Rising Sun: Rising Sun Motor Inn & Cabins, showers

East Glacier: Brownies Hostel, laundry and showers

Polebridge: Polebridge Mercantile, showers

West Glacier: West Glacier KOA, laundry; Laundromat at Canyon Foods in Hungry Horse

Waterton: Showers at townsite campground, but only available to registered campers (including those at Belly River and Crandell Mountain); Waterton Recreation Centre (daily or monthly pass); Bayshore Inn Co-op Laundry

Medical Clinic

West Glacier: West Glacier Clinic, Memorial Day to Labor Day, (406) 888-9924

Post Office

West Glacier: open year-round; closed Saturday, Sunday, and holidays

East Glacier: open year-round; closed Saturday, Sunday, and holidays

St. Mary/Babb: open year-round; closed Saturday, Sunday, and holidays

Waterton: open year-round; closed Saturday, Sunday, and holidays

Gateway Towns

West Entrance

Coram, Hungry Horse, Martin City: 6–10 miles (10–16 km) beyond the West Glacier entrance. The towns of Coram, Hungry Horse, and Martin City make up what is locally called "The Canyon"; lodging, food, and fuel.

Columbia Falls: 17 miles (27 km) from the West Entrance; lodging, food, and fuel. Columbia Falls Chamber of Commerce, 233 13th Street East, Columbia Falls, MT 59912; (406) 892-2072; columbiafallschamber.org.

Kalispell: 33 miles (53 km); airport, lodging, food, fuel, sporting equipment, and hospital. Kalispell Chamber of Commerce, 15 Depot Park, Kalispell, MT 59901; (406) 758-2800; kalispellchamber.org.

Whitefish: 26 miles (42 km); lodging, food, fuel, gift shops, and hospital. Whitefish Chamber of Commerce, 505 Second Street, Whitefish, MT 59937; (406) 862-3501; whitefishchamber.org.

East Glacier / Two Medicine

East Glacier: lodging, food, fuel. East Glacier Chamber of Commerce, 909 MT 49 North, East Glacier Park, MT 59434; (406) 226-4403; eastglacierpark.info.

St. Mary/Many Glacier

St. Mary and Babb: Babb is 5 miles (8 km) from the Many Glacier Road; lodging, food, and fuel. Glacier Country Montana; (800) 338.5072; glaciermt.com.

Browning: Roughly 28 miles (45 km) from the St. Mary entrance along US 89, or 41 miles (66 km) via the Duck Lake Road / MT 464, which is the faster, less curvy route with fewer free-range cows. Blackfeet, Tourism, Parks & Recreation, 16 Old

Person Street, Browning, MT 59417; (406) 338-7406, ext. 2353; blackfeetcountry.com.

Mountain View and Cardston: 18 miles (29 km) and 34 miles (55 km) from Waterton on AB 5; lodging, food, fuel. Cardston and District Chamber of Commerce; (403) 795-1032; cardstontourism.com.

Pincher Creek: 35 miles (56 km) north of Waterton on AB 6; lodging, food, fuel. Pincher Creek Chamber of Commerce; (403) 627-5199; pinchercreek.ca.

Driving Times

Getting Around

Vehicles dominate the summer landscape in Glacier, with the bulk of visitors flocking to Going-to-the-Sun Road. Speeds in Glacier range between 25 mph (40 km/h) to 45 mph (72 km/h). Take a deep breath and enjoy the view for the safety of other drivers, people walking alongside the road, and wildlife.

Sometimes wildlife is the cause of slowdowns along the roadways. To avoid backing up traffic, if there is an animal, slow down and pull over into a parking area, if possible, but don't stop in the middle of the road. If too many people stop to watch, particularly if they are exiting their vehicles, rangers will need to disperse the crowd.

For those who wish to drive at highway speeds in order to make it to one side of the park or the other, opt to take US 2 along the southern boundary, although this is the route recreational vehicles take, so patience is equally important. Recently reconstructed US 89 from Browning to St. Mary is still winding, but wider and smoother. Watch for cows. Montana is a free-range state, which means if you hit a cow, you are liable.

The Akamina and Red Rock Parkways were also completely rehabilitated after the 2017 Kenow Wildfire. Be watchful, as these roads are narrow with blind curves and are used by bicyclists, making it important to be vigilant for people and wildlife.

Driving Times (Approximate)

Going-to-the-Sun Road from West Glacier to St. Mary	50 miles (80 km)	2 hours minimum (without stopping)
North Fork Road from West Entrance to Polebridge	35 miles (56 km)	1 hour
North Fork Road from Polebridge to Kintla	16 miles (26 km)	1 hour
West Glacier to East Glacier	55 miles (89 km)	1–1.5 hours
East Glacier to St. Mary via US 89	44 miles (71 km)	1–1.5 hours
East Glacier to St. Mary via MT 464 (Duck Lake Rd.)	54 miles (87 km)	1–1.5 hours
St. Mary to Many Glacier	20 miles (32 km)	0.75–1 hour
East Glacier to Two Medicine	11 miles (18 km)	0.5 hour
Looking Glass Hwy. (MT 49) from Two Medicine to US 89 south of Cut Bank	12 miles (19 km)	0.5–1 hour
Red Rock Parkway	10 miles (15 km)	1 hour
Akamina Parkway	9.4 miles (15 km)	1 hour
Kalispell to West Glacier	33 miles (53 km)	0.75–1 hour
Great Falls to St. Mary	156 miles (251 km)	2.5–3 hours
St. Mary to Waterton via Cardston, AB	69 miles (111 km)	1.5 hours
St. Mary to Waterton via Chief Mountain Road	43 miles (69 km)	1 hour
Lethbridge, AB, to Waterton	82 miles (132 km)	1.5 hours
Calgary, AB, to Waterton	168 miles (270 km)	3 hours

Safety Notes

Glacier and Waterton Lakes are magical places, but they are not without inherent dangers from natural hazards related to their terrain and inhabitants. Before any outing, spend a couple of moments to think through and prepare for potential situations.

Falling and drowning are the primary reasons for injury or death in the parks. Watch your footing and do not take risks near edges, particularly near water sources, where the rocks might not appear slippery, yet are. The strikingly clear waters of the lakes and rivers are equally inviting, yet shockingly cold and often with very swift currents. Keep a respectful distance from fast-moving streams and rivers, particularly with children, and always wear a life jacket when recreating on any water.

Regardless of the season, dress for nearly any condition. Snow in the summer is not out of the question. Bring an extra layer of clothing and rain gear. In a downpour, it is possible to be sweating one minute, then shaking so badly from cold you can barely function the next. Even on a simple hike, it's normal to sweat when you're walking, then chill down when you stop. Having a fleece or wool layer to pull on until you are moving again is essential.

The sun is intense in this region. Wear a hat and sunglasses, and use sunscreen or protective clothing. Even on short hikes, bring food, and for the love of all that is holy, carry plenty of water. A good rule of thumb is a liter of water for every two hours of a hike, but this increases with temperature and exertion.

Mosquitoes, horseflies, and ticks are prevalent. Wear bug spray, a bug net, or opt for long pants and shirts to help keep them at bay. Be sure to check for ticks during and after your hike.

Glacier and Waterton Lakes are fortunate to be strongholds of the grizzly bear. Hike in groups, preferably of at least four, which is possible even with solo visitors during the height of the summer on busy trails. Carry bear spray, and know how to use it. Trail running is discouraged, since you are traveling quickly and quietly, often through areas with less visibility. Avoid being on the trails before dawn or after sunset to reduce the chances of rousing a bear from a bed or bumping into a traveling bruin. Sing, talk, or yell while hiking, particularly near areas of thick brush or around running water, as well as when it's windy. The human voice is more effective than bear bells or music. There are excellent bear and mountain lion safety recommendations on Glacier's summer backcountry video, nps.gov/glac/learn/photosmultimedia/backcountry-and-bear-safety.htm.

Mountain lions can pose a distinct threat, particularly to pets and children, although encounters are rare. Keep small children close to you on the trail, and in areas where pets are permitted, always have them leashed.

If approached by a mountain lion, make yourself appear large and menacing, and yell and throw things at the cat. Bear spray also works. If a mountain lion attacks, fight as hard as possible, trying to reach the eyes or nose, which are both vulnerable areas.

Moose are fascinating to watch—from a distance. While they appear slow and docile, they move alarmingly fast when agitated, and can shift from calm to irritated in short order. Always give them at least 25 yards (30 m) distance. Be particularly respectful to a cow and calf when you are within their space, and give them room as quickly as possible.

We all love our pets, but dogs (or cats, for that matter) can elicit a negative reaction from wildlife, become prey themselves, as well as be a potential nuisance to other visitors. A deer or moose, particularly with young, is quick to stomp out the potential threat. Small dogs have been taken by mountain lions right in front of their owners. It's best to leave them at home or keep them at a local doggy day-care facility.

Glacier National Park does not allow dogs on the trails, although they are permitted on a leash in campgrounds and around the lodges.

Leashed dogs are permitted on the trails in Waterton Lakes, although Waterton staff also warn visitors of potential human and wildlife conflicts by having your dog in wildlife habitat. Always pick up after your pet.

Hunting is absolutely prohibited within either of the parks, but as of 2010, people who can legally possess a firearm are permitted to carry it in some areas of Glacier National Park, excluding federal facilities such as visitor centers, park offices, and maintenance buildings, along with any private entities that do not allow them. It is illegal to display a firearm in a threatening manner or fire it. Since numerous reputable studies indicate that bear spray is far more effective in stopping a bear or mountain lion attack, carrying bear spray as a nonlethal deterrent is a smarter choice.

Firearms may be transported in Waterton Lakes National Park, as long as they are unloaded and in their case. They may not be taken out of the vehicle.

How to Use This Guide

Common and Scientific Names

The primary goal of this guide is to give readers the confidence to have a solid idea as to what they observe, whether it's a flower, bird, plant, or insect. If someone can tell the difference between a lupine and a blue camas, or a coyote and a wolf, it is a success. In this guide, we offer the family name, along with the more-specific genus and species for most of the entries. Since some species' differences are quite subtle, a few entries contain simply the more-general names. While every effort was made to provide the current status of every species within this book, new discoveries change names and families. To stay abreast of the most up-to-date information, check out the Integrated Taxonomic Information System, itis.gov.

Photo Tips

It's practically impossible to take a bad photo in Glacier and Waterton Lakes National Parks. One of the best pieces of advice if you're looking for exceptional images is to not rely on your phone camera. A digital single-lens reflex (SLR) camera with interchangeable lenses offers the greatest latitude, although there are some point-and-shoot digital cameras with helpful features that can produce high-quality images.

For a few technical tips, consider keeping the aperture setting in the midrange, around f/8 to f/11, to create depth and maintain sharpness. Also, remember to set the ISO (your camera's sensitivity to light) between 100 and 400 during the day to prevent the photos from turning out too grainy. Investing in a polarizing filter can make the already brilliant colors pop.

One of the best reasons for using an SLR while visiting Glacier and Waterton Lakes is the ability to attach a telephoto lens to photograph wildlife. The minimum telephoto length you'll want is a 300mm, although for birds and many mammals, having a 400mm to 600mm lens makes a world of difference.

Tips for Wildlife Viewing in Glacier and Waterton Lakes

Pick your season: Choosing the time of year that best lines up with what you want to photograph is your first step in planning. May and June are great for babies. Wildflowers are stunning in the spring and early summer, and this is the prime time for birds. In July and August everything is maturing, yet beautiful flowers are still found in the higher elevations. As August wanes, autumn graces the parks with bright colors and cooler temperatures. Birds have left, or are still leaving, yet it's a good time to see bears, coyotes, foxes, elk, and moose. Winter is the quiet time, although there is still plenty to see. Look for waterfowl congregating in the open waters. Raptors often are more visible during these colder months, and it's still a terrific time to view deer, bighorn sheep, elk, and moose.

Have the right tools: It's handy to have a pair of binoculars to glass slopes and other areas, looking for birds or wildlife. A spotting scope on a tripod is an even more powerful tool, allowing you to watch wildlife at greater distances.

Choose the quiet time: When looking for wildlife, head out early or stay out long after everyone else goes back to camp for dinner. The roads are far less congested during these times, and it's easier to cover more miles looking for animals.

Stay safe: Always be respectful when photographing wildlife. Besides maintaining the legal distances of 100 yards (100 m) for bears and 25 yards (30 m) for deer, elk, and other wildlife, never block an animal's path if it wants to cross a road or area. Don't feed animals to bring them closer, and do not yell or make noises to encourage them to look in your direction.

Suggested Nature Hikes and Wildlife Viewing Areas

Glacier and Waterton Lakes are a hiker's paradise, and it takes an entire book to find the best adventures. A longtime favorite guide to the trails within the parks is FalconGuides' *Hiking Glacier and Waterton Lakes National Parks* by Erik Molvar. The best map to display the hiking options is Hike 734's (hike734.com) *Day Hiking in Glacier National Park* by Jake Bramante, where he highlights popular routes.

Everyone wants to see a grizzly, at least from a safe distance, when they visit Glacier and Waterton Lakes, but there are many interesting characters beyond this charismatic megafauna. From entertaining ground squirrels to majestic golden eagles, there are limitless opportunities to experience every aspect of wildlife in the parks.

When and where to see wildlife is not an exact science, but a good place to start is checking in at any of the visitor centers or ranger stations. They can help you figure out where to find the different species you're hoping to see, and they will also offer warnings for potentially dangerous situations.

A coyote in the fields around St. Mary Lake

1. **North Fork:** The North Fork is home to all of the predators within the park, as there are ample mule deer and elk in the area. Due to several fires over the past three decades, the remaining snags are an exceptional habit for woodpeckers, including American three-toed, downy, and pileated. Other birds, such as ravens, nuthatches, mountain chickadees, western tanagers, and many more are found in these areas. On the waters of Bowman and Kintla Lakes, you can frequently spot common loons, common mergansers, and common goldeneyes.

    Polebridge is a quaint mountain town with good food and a welcoming atmosphere, and the jumping-off point to explore Bowman and Kintla Lakes. Even though the road leading back to both of these areas is narrow, bumpy, and dusty, they are exceptionally busy during the summer, causing the park to limit visitation. Much of the hiking is through the trees, but Numa Ridge Lookout offers terrific views, and the Quartz Lake Loop is a moderate hike, starting at Bowman Lake and reaching Quartz Lake before returning to Bowman.

2. **Lake McDonald:** As throughout the park, both species of bears are present in this area. Black bears are typically more visible along the roadsides, and grizzlies are sometimes spotted in the avalanche slopes in the early spring. White-tailed deer frequent the roadsides and campgrounds around West Glacier and Apgar, and because of their presence, always remember that mountain lions are most likely there as well. Ground squirrels chirp from many grassy areas, and white-crowned sparrows and Steller's jays frequent the forests. Lake McDonald teems with waterfowl, including common loons, western grebes, common mergansers, coots, mallards, and bufflehead. Upper McDonald Creek has the highest number of harlequin duck pairs in the park.

    An easy hike along Upper McDonald Creek takes you through lush growth reminiscent of the Pacific Northwest, with ferns, lichen, and enormous firs and hemlocks. John's

The view at Lake McDonald

Lake Loop is a simple stroll, particularly for families, and Avalanche Lake is the most popular hike in the park. Keep this in mind, as finding a parking spot can be practically impossible after eight a.m. during the summer. For a more-rigorous day, head to Mount Brown Lookout or Sperry Chalet, where you can order lunch or a piece of pie at the dining room to reward your hard work.

3. **Going-to-the-Sun Road/Logan Pass:** Traveling into the alpine territory increases the possibility of more wildlife sightings. Grizzlies are sometimes spotted across the valley on distant slopes, and at times are as close as the meadows around Logan Pass, digging for either ground squirrels or glacier lily corms. Mountain goats are common around the visitor center, but maintain a respectful distance of at least 25 yards (10 m). Bighorn sheep are also often seen on the surrounding slopes. For a few lucky souls, this is a good place to possibly even see a wolverine.

Hiking to Hidden Lake, or even as far as the Hidden Lake Overlook, pays off with gorgeous scenery, as well as possibly spotting mountain goats and bighorn sheep along the way. The trail heading down to the lake is closed during cutthroat trout spawning to give grizzlies their space, but the overlook is a perfect stop. The Highline Trail to Granite Park is a popular trail for good reason. It's 7.2 miles (12 km) of stunning views all the way to Granite Park Chalet, through subalpine meadows filled with wildflowers. From Granite Park Chalet, the shortest route is the 4 miles (6 km) down to the Loop, the hairpin section on Going-to-the-Sun Road. For those looking for a longer day with fewer people, consider Gunsight Lake. At just over 12 miles (19 km) round-trip, and roughly a 1,500' (457 m) elevation gain, the views from the lake are worth every step.

4. **US 2 Corridor / Essex / Marias Pass:** Pull off in the turnouts to scan the slopes on the other side of the Flathead River for elk, deer, and bears. Sometimes river otters and beavers are found in the water below. Visit the parking area at the Goat Lick to watch the goats clinging to the cliff as they lick the minerals on the rock face. As the landscape opens up closer to Marias Pass, look for moose in the wetlands. Wolves sometimes even cruise through the area. In the forest, martins hunt small prey such as flying squirrels, and mountain chickadees, dark-eyed juncos, and cedar waxwings spend the summer here.

   From the Walton Ranger Station, the manned Scalplock Lookout is a steady uphill climb rewarded with stunning views of Mount St. Nicholas, including an amazing perspective from the outhouse. If you're hiking in June or July, expect chest-high bear grass and lush vegetation.

5. **East Glacier / Two Medicine:** It's not out of the question to see grizzlies and black bears on the golf course in East Glacier, particularly in the early mornings. Badgers prey upon the ground squirrels in the area, and are known to waddle across the manicured lawn of the Glacier Park Lodge. In Two

Rising Wolf Mountain in the Two Medicine area

Medicine, glass the slopes of Rising Wolf and the surrounding mountains to spot bighorn sheep and mountain goats. Moose are frequent visitors in Pray Lake, Two Medicine Lake, Upper Two Medicine Lake, Cobalt Lake, and any of the ponds along the way. Look for beavers and yellow-headed blackbirds in many of these same areas. In the forest listen for warbling vireos, song sparrows, and ruffed grouse drumming in the woods. On the water, look for common loons, buffleheads, cinnamon teals, and lesser scaups.

Hiking around East Glacier requires a Blackfeet Tribal Conservation Permit, but it is not required within Two Medicine. The trail to Scenic Point takes hikers through the skeletal remains of whitebark pines killed by blister rust. A dramatically different landscape, the hike to Cobalt Lake is filled with lush wildflowers and wildlife. Hoary marmots at the lake are not shy, but do not feed them. For those who wish to stay closer to the water, trails on either side of Two Medicine Lake offer easy and tranquil hikes. You can also take the boat from the Glacier Park Boat Company across

Two Medicine Lake to continue hiking for the day, including the long route over Dawson Pass.

6. **St. Mary:** There's always something interesting to find in St. Mary, from grizzlies in the open meadows to black bears emerging from the shrubs along St. Mary Lake. Coyotes hunt the open grasslands for ground squirrels, and foxes are often seen trotting along the roadways or the edges of aspen groves. Moose frequent the areas around the lake, moving into the aspens or trees to find respite. Two Dog Flats is the best place to see elk in the area, particularly in the autumn, although it's equally good for bears when the copious chokecherries and serviceberries are ripe. Killdeer nest in the gravel areas of pullouts and campgrounds, and red-winged blackbirds reside in the reeds near the beaver ponds. On St. Mary Lake look for common loons and Barrow's goldeneyes, along with ospreys and bald eagles and, once in a while, the American white pelican.

     Easy hikes around St. Mary include the 3-mile (5 km) loop to the Beaver Ponds, where you can expect to see meadows filled with wildflowers and birdlife throughout the previously burned areas. For those who love waterfalls, see three on your hike to St. Mary Falls. For a longer day, head to Otokomi Lake from the trailhead near Rising Sun. There are a few waterfalls along the way, and the lake is positioned in a beautiful area.

7. **Many Glacier:** Surrounded by open slopes, Many Glacier is a good area to glass for grizzlies and black bears. During the summer season, interpretive rangers set up spotting scopes most nights of the week in the Swiftcurrent Motor Inn parking area to look for bears and bighorn sheep on the slope behind the complex. Moose are common in Swiftcurrent, Fishercap, and Red Rock Lakes. On any trail within the Many Glacier valley, look for bears, bighorn sheep, and mountain goats along the mountain slopes. Red squirrels

and chipmunks are common in the forest, along with ruffed and spruce grouse. In the higher elevations, listen for ptarmigans clucking along the trail.

Some of the best hiking happens in Many Glacier. Iceberg Lake, Ptarmigan Tunnel, and Grinnell Glacier are enormously popular, and the trails are rarely quiet during the summer. Cracker Lake is renowned for its surreal aquamarine color that comes from the glacial silt. Even a simple stroll around Swiftcurrent Lake provides exceptional views, and a walk along Josephine Lake is a good way to see moose and bears.

8. **Waterton:** You don't have to go far to immerse yourself in wildlife in Waterton. Bighorn sheep and mule deer are town residents. Black bears also visit town, as well as the open slopes and alongside the parkway roads and campgrounds when the berries ripen. Elk, mule deer, and white-tailed deer are more likely found in the aspen groves and grasslands, and watch for northern flickers and western meadowlarks. The Maskinonge is a unique wetland and a haven for birdlife. Look for tundra and trumpeter swans and myriad waterfowl that bring the area to life in the spring. It's also a good spot for common mergansers, common goldeneyes, sandhill cranes, and blue-winged teals. Raptors and owls take advantage of this area with its abundance of small prey, and the eastern section of Waterton is a known golden eagle migration route in the fall.

The most memorable hike in Waterton is the Crypt Lake Trail. Start by taking the boat shuttle across Upper Waterton Lake to the trailhead; then it's just a matter of climbing a ladder, crawling through the tunnel, and hanging on to the chain as you make your way along a cliff. (This excursion isn't for those who are afraid of heights!) Bertha Falls and Lake is much less harrowing, with the trail at a much lower elevation the entire way. Even for those walking around town, Cameron Falls is an easy stroll for practically everyone.

For wildlife watchers, drive the Red Rock and Akamina Parkways early in the morning and around dusk, or spend the afternoon canoeing, paddleboating, or kayaking at Cameron Lake before continuing the search for wildlife. The Bison Paddock, which was closed in 2017 due to the Kenow Wildfire, traditionally houses roughly half a dozen bison to represent the massive herds that once roamed this region. There is a loop drive within the paddock that sometimes brings you close to the animals, but please remember that they are still wild, and remain in your vehicle at all times.

Natural Areas Outside Glacier and Waterton Lakes National Parks

1. **Bob Marshall Wilderness Complex:** Glacier doesn't stand alone in the ecosystem. Beyond its southern border, the Bob Marshall Wilderness Complex encompasses more than 1.5 million acres (607,028.5 ha). Access the BMWC from a number of trailheads surrounding the area, although Spotted Bear in the Flathead National Forest is the closest to Glacier and Waterton Lakes. Flathead National Forest Supervisor's Office, 650 Wolfpack Way, Kalispell, MT; (406) 758-5208; usda.gov/attmain/flathead/specialplaces.

2. **Hungry Horse Dam and Reservoir:** Engineering minds and outdoor enthusiasts enjoy visiting the Hungry Horse Dam and recreating in and around Hungry Horse Reservoir. The area is popular for boating, kayaking, fishing, water-skiing, and swimming, along with hiking, off-road recreation, and huckleberry picking. Camping is open on Forest Service land, and there is the Spotted Bear Campground, 55 miles south of Hungry Horse along the bumpy and dusty East Side Reservoir Road #38. As within Glacier and Waterton Lakes, always store your food properly to avoid bear conflict. Hungry Horse Ranger District; (406) 387-3800; fs.usda.gov/recarea/flathead/recarea/?recid=66838. From Memorial Day

weekend to Labor Day, the visitor center at the dam is open to tours and interpretative programs; (406) 387-5241; visit mt.com/listings/general/lake/hungry-horse-reservoir.html.

3. **National Bison Range:** A couple of hours south of West Glacier in Moise, the National Bison Range, established by President Theodore Roosevelt in 1908 to assist in the preservation of the bison, gives visitors a chance to drive through the 18,500-acre (7,487 ha) reserve. Not only home to bison, visitors also see a diversity of wildlife, including pronghorn antelope, elk, mule deer, white-tailed deer, and bighorn sheep, along with coyotes and badgers (both of the latter hunt the prolific Columbian ground squirrels); 58355 Bison Range Road; Moiese, MT 59824; (406) 644-2211; fws.gov/refuge/National_Bison_Range/.

4. **Flathead Lake:** Located an hour and a half from West Glacier, Flathead Lake is the largest natural freshwater lake west of the Mississippi. With 160 miles (257.5 km) of shoreline, this clear, deep lake is a paradise for water lovers. And if you're lucky, you'll catch a glimpse of the elusive Flathead Lake Monster! Flathead Convention and Visitor Bureau; (406) 756-9091; https://www.fcvb.org/flathead-lake-montana.php.

5. **Sun River Wildlife Management Area and Sun Canyon:** If the crowds ever become too much at Glacier, the Sun River Wildlife Management Area and Sun Canyon are only three hours from West Glacier and just over two hours from St. Mary. The nearly 20,000-acre (8,094 ha) game range is the winter ground for thousands of elk that move between there and the Bob Marshall Wilderness Complex, as well as home to grizzlies, black bears, mountain lions, and bighorn sheep. The game range is open for travel from May 15 through November 30; (406) 467-2488; https://myfwp.mt .gov/fwPub/landsMgmt/siteDetail.action?lmsId=39753612. Gibson Reservoir is the 6-mile-long (10-km-long) reservoir

at the end of the road that winds past the Sun River Management Area and through the picturesque Sun Canyon. With several Forest Service campgrounds in the area, this is a destination spot for many locals. And for those who want to grab a burger, or stay at a campground with showers and laundry facilities, check out the Sun Canyon Lodge at (406) 562-3654; suncanyonlodge.com.

6. **Freezeout Lake:** In the late fall and again in the early to mid-spring, tens of thousands of migrating waterfowl take center stage at Freezeout Lake, especially the swans and snow geese that arrive in droves. Only two hours from East Glacier via US 89, these shallow waters teem with birdlife; (406) 467-2488; myfwp.mt.gov/fwpPub/landsMgmt/siteDetail.action?lmsId=39753612.

7. **Head-Smashed-In Buffalo Jump:** An hour north of Waterton Lakes, the Head-Smashed-In Buffalo Jump offers a glimpse into the world of indigenous peoples thousands of years ago. A World Heritage Site, Head-Smashed-In explains the harsh realities of obtaining life's necessities by depending upon the massive herds of bison that once roamed the grasslands of North America; (403) 553-2731; headsmashedin.ca.

8. **Banff National Park:** Four to five hours from Waterton, Banff National Park is one of the shining jewels in the Canadian Rockies. This contemporary town is a hub of activity, with world-class shopping, excellent food, and luxurious accommodations. Home to grizzlies, black bears, wolves, elk, and moose, Banff is an excellent place to watch wildlife; (403) 762-1550; pc.gc.ca/en/pn-np/ab/banff.

Ecosystems

The unique habitats on either side of the Continental Divide share stories of the progression of the environment. The lushness of the western side is due to the greater amounts of moisture from

Pacific systems, resulting in dense, varied, and, in some cases, ancient forests. Lodgepole pines spring up where fire cleared earlier trees and brush, creating thick "doghair"-type stands that are void of significant undergrowth. Over centuries, lodgepole stands are eventually succeeded by climax species such as firs and spruce, ultimately creating an environment where flowering plants, fungi, and shrubs such as snowberries and huckleberries thrive. These habitats are found throughout the North Fork region in Glacier, as well as any of the post-fire areas.

The 500-year-old giants along the Trail of the Cedars near Lake McDonald are a testament to this succession, with the dominant western hemlock, western red cedar, and enormous black cottonwoods shading out many of the smaller shrubby specimens. Only deep shade–loving plants, particularly those that don't have to photosynthesize, thrive in this realm.

As the elevation increases above 6,000' (1,829 m), even old trees don't have the massiveness of the aged hemlocks and red cedars. In this area, the extreme winds and years of heavy snow cause Engelmann spruce, subalpine fir, and whitebark pine to sometimes grow stunted and gnarled, exhibiting what is called krummholz, which is German for "crooked wood." The rocky landscape is interspersed with short, spreading plants that make the most of the extraordinarily short season. Vegetation that takes hold in this region has a compressed but spectacular life cycle similar to arctic vegetation communities. This is also the realm of the remaining glaciers as they continue their slow movement grinding through the mountain landscape. Snow-covered for the most part, the twenty-six remaining glaciers are eventually melting into beautiful high-backcountry lakes.

Waterton Lakes is often referred to as the land "where the mountains meet the prairie," and the story of the region starts in the grasslands that once were home to vast herds of bison. In both Waterton Lakes and the east side of Glacier around St. Mary, the prairie stretches out from the mountain foothills. There are still many areas with productive fir and spruce forests, but mixed forests and aspen groves are more prevalent than thick stands of lodgepole pines or the old growth of the west side. In the grassy expanse of the prairie landscape, bunchgrasses and pockets of shrubs such as silverberry and chokecherry grow in thickets as protection from the notorious winds, and to make the best use of water sources.

Geology

Long before the glaciers crowned the mountains, mighty forces shaped the landscape in a complex geological story. Millions of years ago, an enormous inland sea covered parts of Montana, Idaho, Washington, and southwestern Canada, settling sediment upon the seafloor. As a result, much of the rock within Glacier and Waterton Lakes demonstrates this layering effect, as well as the forces of the water, including rippling from the settling and wave actions of the shallow, ancient inland sea still seen within the sedimentary rock.

Throughout these millennia, heat from the lava below and pressure from the continual sedimentation above created quartzite, argillite, and several other metamorphic types of rock. Many of these, which began as the lower layers of the process, were folded,

The view of Jackson Glacier from the Jackson Glacier Overlook

flipped, and pushed upward and eastward when the subterranean plates collided approximately 150 to 160 million years ago, in what is referred to as the Lewis Overthrust. As a result, many of the visible rocks are 1.6 billion years old.

In this timeline, the glaciers are relative newcomers that were formed a couple of million years ago during the most recent ice age. Scientists believe they were present, and many persisted, during a warming period in the Holocene epoch roughly six thousand years ago, and rebounded during the Little Ice Age, between 1770 and 1840, before beginning their retreat by the mid-1800s.

In 1850, roughly 150 glaciers clung to the upper elevations. As of 2020, only 26 glaciers remain. While Waterton Lakes was shaped by the same forces, no glaciers remain in the park.

Glacier NPS

WESTERN TOAD
Anaxyrus boreas
Toad family (Bufonidae)
Quick ID: Olive green to brown; covered in bumps of various sizes that are darker than the rest of the body; light stripe down back
Length: 3–5" (8–13 cm)

A species of special concern in Montana, partially due to the presence of a type of chytrid fungi that results in a skin condition affecting the toad's respiration. To battle the fungus, researchers speculate that affected amphibians bask in the sun for longer periods to reduce the severity of the infection, although they are quick to seek refuge under a log or in some sort of burrow when the temperature climbs. These toads are primarily nocturnal, hunting beetles, ants, millipedes, and spiders, but are spotted during the day from low-elevation wetlands to higher talus slopes. The bumps on the toad are called warts, and the light stripe down the back of adults is an easy field mark.

COLUMBIA SPOTTED FROG
Rana luteiventris
True Frog family (Ranidae)
Quick ID: Olive green to light brown with darker spots and markings; bright pink-salmon to reddish color on belly and underneath legs; bumps on the back
Length: 2–3.5" (5–9 cm)

Found in the ponds, springs, and backwaters, sometimes created by beaver dams, in open forests and sunnier areas, the Columbia spotted frog is often confused with leopard or wood frogs. Breeding takes place between mid-April and June, with the males moving to ponds or shallow areas of lakes where there is plenty of vegetation for cover. The resulting floating globules of several hundred eggs hatch into tadpoles within three weeks. The tadpoles are vulnerable to fish and voracious dragonfly larvae, and even adult frogs need to watch out for garter snakes and birds. Adults feed during both the day and night on insects, earthworms, snails, and spiders. At the end of the season, the frogs hunker down in the muck or squeeze themselves into a protected crevice to spend the winter.

LONG-TOED SALAMANDER
Ambystoma macrodactylum
Mole Salamander family (Ambystomatidae)
Quick ID: Dark coloration with bright yellow to tan or olive-green stripe down the back
Length: 3–4" (8–10 cm)

Inhabitants of lower-elevation lakes and the surrounding old-growth regions, as well as mixed forest stands, long-toed salamanders are at home in these lush, rich habitats. These sleek, often black amphibians are named as such because the fourth toe on their hind feet is longer than the others. More prominent on the west side of the Continental Divide, they're more visible in the early spring during the breeding season, when they spend up to a month near a small pond or shallow water. Maturing at two to three years old, they return to the general area where they were born to breed and lay eggs, and it may take two to fourteen months to mature and eventually move to upland areas. Their primary food sources include millipedes, spiders, insects, and caddisfly larvae. During the winter they tuck themselves into rodent burrows, as well as under rocks or logs, to hibernate.

WESTERN PAINTED TURTLE
Chrysemys picta bellii
Pond Turtle family (Emydidae)
Quick ID: Smooth, dark shell, sometimes lined with yellow or red lining shields or along edges; brightly colored red or yellow-orange on belly
Length: 3–10" (8–25 cm)

The western painted is the only turtle found in Glacier, and is a protected species within Waterton Lakes. They are most often spotted basking on shorelines or upon half-submerged logs in ponds or lakes, and although they seem unaware, they quickly scoot into the water if approached. Being omnivores, they feed upon small fish, insects, tadpoles, and aquatic vegetation. The females don't begin breeding until they're six to seven years old, when they lay four to fifteen soft-shelled oval eggs in a hole she digs in the sandy or gravelly soil. Afterward, she buries her nest and heads back to the water. The eggs are vulnerable to skunks, raccoons, otters, and weasels, and it's up to the young to find their own way to safety when they hatch.

Please note that even though many of the mushrooms in Glacier and Waterton Lakes National Parks are edible, it is illegal to harvest them within either of the parks.

BLACK MOREL
Morchella elata
Morel family (Morchellaceae)
Quick ID: Honeycombed, elongated cap; may be light brown, but often darkens with age; cap is attached to the lighter stem; cap and stem are hollow
Height: 2–10" (5–25 cm)

Like robins, morels are a sign of spring in this region, as they often appear first along the south-facing slopes as the sun warms the cold soil. Although there are at least twenty-one species of morels in North America, there are only three to four in Montana and Alberta, including the white (also called natural) morels, *Morchella deliciosa*, found in yards and urban areas, and yellow morels, *Morchella esculenta*, which thrive around cottonwoods in this region. The black morels are closely associated with conifer forests, particularly after fires. True morels are distinguished by their honeycomb texture and, most importantly, the hollow interior throughout. All are edible, as long as they are well cooked to reduce chances of food poisoning, but it is important to remember that it's illegal to harvest any mushrooms within either of the parks.

RED BAND BRACKET
Fomitopsis pinicola
Fomitopsidaceae family (Fomitopsidaceae)
Quick ID: Grows horizontally; dark brown; reddish to light-colored bands
Size: 3–16" (8–41 cm) long by 0.5–4" (1–10 cm) tall

When walking through conifer forests, check closely at the dead trees for shelf-like protrusions emerging from the trunks. The red band bracket, a type of polypore mushroom with a multitude of tiny pores on the underside instead of gills, is a key player in breaking down the cellulose of the trees. What remains is the deep brown, cube-like lignin that is processed by a different fungus. This shelf-type fungus starts out as a lighter cream color when it's young, gradually darkening as it matures, creating bands of new growth. The edge is typically light with a red band next to it, and its age can be estimated by the number of these growth layers. The texture on the top feels woody, while underneath it is made up of light-colored, soft pores that often drip a liquid.

HORSE HOOF POLYPORE
Fomes fomentarius
Polypore family (Polyporaceae)
Quick ID: Gray to brown; narrow to chunkier, hooflike shape
Size: 2–8" (5–20 cm) wide by 1–8" (3–20 cm) tall

While the red band bracket focuses on conifers, the horse hoof polypore is found mostly on birch trees in the region. With older specimens, it's easy to see how this polypore acquired its descriptive common name, since it resembles a horse's hoof. Another interesting common name is the tinder polypore, as this species has a history in fire-making in the millennia before matches. When the fibrous layers within the mushroom are cut out and fluffed to make tinder, they easily catch a spark; plus the hard yet porous nature of the outside of the fungi kept embers smoldering for extended periods of time. This particular type was found among the belongings of Ötzi, the mummified Ice Man found in the Alps in 1991, as either a fire starter or part of his medicinal cache.

OYSTER MUSHROOMS
Pleurotus spp.
Pleurotaceae family (Pleurotaceae)
Quick ID: White to cream-colored; grows in shelflike layers on the tree; white gills; oyster shell shape
Length: 1–10" (3–25 cm)

Large cottonwoods remain stately sentinels in the forest long after they die, which is why it's difficult to miss the bright white oyster mushrooms growing in overlapping shelves along these massive specimens. Named oyster mushrooms because of their appearance, not their flavor, they look similar to a large shell. With a very mild flavor, they are a favorite cultivated variety commercially or at home, as well as one that is harvested outside the parks. Oyster mushrooms are smooth on the top and have distinct gills, yet do not have a stalklike stem like other mushrooms. Instead, they seemingly stretch outward and upward from the bark itself. They have a pleasant fragrance similar to licorice. When it comes to the *Pleurotus* genus, researchers are constantly discovering new aspects of their nutritional and medicinal benefits. *Pleurotus populinus, Pleurotus ostreatus,* and *Pleurotus pulmonarius,* which are sometimes called the *Pleurotus* complex of *P. ostreatus-pulmonarius,* all share similar properties.

PANTHER AMANITA
Amanita pantherina
Amanita family (Amanitaceae)

Quick ID: Light yellowish-brown to brown; rounded cap often with white "warts" on the top; white to off-white gills do not attach to the stem; white spore print; ring around the rather thick (0.4–1" [1–2.5 cm]) white stem

Height: 2–5" (6–12 cm)

Part of a large family, what is called *Amanita pantherina* in North America is genetically distinct from its European counterpart of the same name. Found in older conifer forests in partial shade, particularly during the summer, the panther amanita looks like an egg emerging from the duff before it breaks through the soft soil and plant litter to form the classic rounded cap with white warts. It grows 2–4" (5–9 cm) wide and flattens as it ages. The partial veil, which is the thin membrane covering the gills as it emerges, pulls away and leaves a ring around the stem, a distinguishing characteristic of the amanitas. Even though many amanitas are deadly to people, squirrels and other animals eat them without ill effects.

43

YELLOW CORAL
Ramaria spp.
Gomphaceae family (Gomphaceae)
Quick ID: Off-white to pale-yellowish-, salmon-, or orange-colored; resembles cauliflower
Height: 3–6" (7–15 cm) by 2–6" (5–15 cm) wide

When it looks like there is cauliflower—or an alien being—emerging from the duff of an older conifer forest, it is the common yellow coral, or one of its relatives, making its early summer appearance. Starting with a cream-colored hue sporting off-white stems, this unique looking mushroom matures to a more-yellowish, orange, or salmon color, and highly resembles a prickly-looking cauliflower. Different varieties bruise brown or blue when they are squeezed. While some spring coral mushrooms are edible for people (harvested outside the park), there are several varieties that are poisonous and cause potentially serious gastrointestinal distress. The multiple crevices are favorite spaces for insects, and squirrels depend on all sorts of mushrooms, including these tasty yellow corals, and are key to spreading the spores of the fungi.

PIXIE CUPS
Cladonia spp.
Cladoniaceae family (Cladoniaceae)
Quick ID: Blue-green to gray; resembles tiny golf tees
Height: 0.5–1" (1–3 cm)

Lichens—a combination of fungi and algae, or fungi, algae, and a cyanobacteria—are fascinating specimens, and are sometimes referred to as the "fungus that discovered agriculture." There are dozens of pixie cup lichen varieties in Montana and Alberta, and while there might be differences both on the physiological and genetic levels, they share many similarities. Most of these intricate looking lichens appear as miniature worlds where the fairy-size goblet-like structures emerge from a green and often dusty foundation. Pixie cups are a combination of crustose and foliose lichens, sharing the characteristics of both. Like many other lichens, one means of reproduction involves forming a cluster of a few cells of algae combined with fungi cells to form a soredium. Although it looks like a small grain of sand, it contains all the pixie cup needs to start a new group of this adorable lichen.

EDIBLE HORSEHAIR LICHEN
Bryoria fremontii
Parmeliaceae family (Parmeliaceae)
Quick ID: Dark brown; fine and stringy strands
Length: 10–12" (25–30 cm)

The long, dark strands of dry lichen hanging throughout the forests of Glacier and Waterton Lakes might give an eerie appearance, but the edible horsehair lichen has long been an important food for indigenous people, boiled into a jellylike substance that is eaten with other foods or dried for storage. It's also eaten by some wildlife and used as nest-building material for birds. Recent discoveries of the horsehair lichen expand the understanding of its complex makeup. Although horsehair lichen is made up of exactly the same fungi and algae combination as the tortured horsehair lichen, *Bryoria tortuosa*, the latter is bright greenish-yellow and contains vulpinic acid, a toxic compound also found in the distinct wolf lichen. Montana lichenologist Toby Spribille learned that a particular yeast, a basidiomycete yeast to be exact, made the difference in the characteristics of these two similar species, explaining why one is edible and the other is poisonous.

LAPLAND BEARD LICHEN
Usnea lapponica
Parmeliaceae family (Parmeliaceae)
Quick ID: Gray to pale green-gray; shrubby; irregularly shaped
Length: 1–5" (2–12 cm)

The Lapland beard lichen, also called powdered beard lichen, is one member of the very large group of *Usnea* found throughout North America and the world. This is one of the most prominent species in the parks, clinging onto the bark and branches of the trees in mixed conifer forests on either side of the Continental Divide. Sometimes it hangs down from the branches, while other times you'll see it perched upright on the stems. Worldwide, there is a long history of the medicinal uses for the *Usnea* species. It's well-known for its antiseptic and antifungal properties. Historic methods of use included applying the entire plant to a wound, crushing it into a powder to administer to a particular area, or steeped as a tincture or infusion to treat respiratory infections.

WOLF LICHEN
Letharia vulpina
Parmeliaceae family (Parmeliaceae)
Quick ID: Chartreuse or bright yellow-green; shrubby appearance
Height: 1–2" (3–5 cm)

Wolf lichen is the bright green, bristly specimen clinging to trunks and branches of dead conifers throughout the parks. The neon coloration is hard to miss on the mature trees. Although there is chlorophyll from the algae for photosynthesis, the bright green is due to the presence of vulpinic acid, a potent poison. In Europe at least as far back as the mid-1700s, the lichen—which is named "vulpina" in reference to foxes, whose scientific name is *Vulpes vulpes*—was ground up into a powder and sprinkled on meat (sometimes mixed with glass) to kill both foxes and wolves. There's a question as to whether the lichen or glass actually killed the animals, although indigenous people in North America are also known to have tipped arrows with the powdered poison. The brightly colored lichen was also used to create a brilliant yellow dye for porcupine quills and other materials by the Salish, Kootenai, and Blackfeet people.

REINDEER LICHEN
Cladonia rangiferina
Cladoniaceae family (Cladoniaceae)
Quick ID: Gray to gray-green; highly branched, small and shrublike; hollow stems; forms rounded clumps
Height: 1–4" (3–10 cm)

It can be easy to overlook the mats of these gray or gray-green tiny, shrubby lichens growing in small patches or rounded cushions covering slopes in the older conifer forests. They thrive despite arid conditions, obtaining the moisture and nutrients they need from the air, with the algae part of the lichen producing sugars through photosynthesis. They are more whitish-gray when they are dry, but green up quickly with ample moisture. This particular lichen prefers sunnier conditions, and is seen in open areas with minimal shading. Reindeer lichen reproduces asexually when pieces are knocked off or dispersed by voles or other rodents, although they also reproduce through spores that travel on the wind to form a new colony. This species is common in Canada and the northern tier of the United States, and is an important winter forage for caribou in the arctic regions.

LUNGWORT
Lobaria pulmonaria
Lobariaceae family (Lobariaceae)
Quick ID: Green to gray; scalloped, wavy, large-lobed, leaflike structures
Size: 4–12" (10–30 cm)

The lobed appearance is indicative of its name, as it resembles lungs clinging to the old trees. This foliose (leaflike) lichen utilizes the algae to photosynthesize nutrients and the dark patches of cyanobacteria on the underpart of the structure to capture nitrogen from the atmosphere. When lungwort falls from the trees, the nitrogen present in the lichen works its way into the soil, ultimately supplying nitrogen to the trees and plants around it. Lungworts reproduce mainly by forming clumps of soredia, a group of fungal and algal cells, located on the top of the lichen. When these fall off, or are swept away by wind or the disturbance of animals, they form new lichens, if conditions are right. Sometimes they'll also create apothecia, open cup or saucer-shaped structures that make up a fruiting body for the lichen.

FRIGHTENED CAT-TAIL MOSS
Rhytidiadelphus triquetrus
Hylocomiaceae family (Hylocomiaceae)
Quick ID: Green to greenish-yellow; brushy look; red stems with small branches; grows in mats; leaves are up to 0.25" (6 mm) long
Height: 2–6" (5–15 cm)

Also called rough goose neck moss or the even more descriptive electrified cat's tail moss, these names paint the picture of the flaring leaves of this dainty moss. Although diminutive, this short specimen with its red stem and the tiny 0.1–0.2" (3–5 mm) main leaves growing every which way, just like a frightened cat's tail, it's easy to spot even on a mossy bank. Overall, it appears loose and a little unkempt. The frightened cat-tail moss is one of the most prominent species in the forests of Glacier and Waterton Lakes, as it prefers the environment within the abundant conifer forests of the region. There are specific male and female parts on separate plants. It grows better with some sunshine, but needs fairly consistent moisture.

JUNIPER HAIRCAP MOSS
Polytrichum juniperinum
Branching Mosses family (Polytrichaceae)
Quick ID: Green, slender, pointy leaves flare out from center; brown-reddish stems
Height: 0.4–2" (1–5 cm)

This prolific and prevalent moss looks like ancient trees blanketing a miniature landscape. It is fully appreciated when viewed up close, so don't hesitate to bend down with a hand lens or use a phone to zoom into the intricacies of this beautiful specimen. Juniper haircap moss grows in coniferous forests in lower to subalpine regions, and tends to lean toward drier, marginal soils. They produce asexually through stems touching the soil, or the rhizoids—which are the tiny rootlike hairs at the bottom of the structure—to form a new plant, as well as sexually through spore production. The yellow to reddish-brown male reproductive organs, called antheridia, look like tiny flowers on the top of the stems, and the resulting sporophytes boast beige capsules on the top of slender brown stems that stand tall above the rest of the moss.

STAIRSTEP MOSS
Hylocomium splendens
Hylocomiaceae family (Hylocomiaceae)
Quick ID: Olive green to yellowish-green; feathery leaves on zigzagging, branched red stems 0.08–0.1" (2–3 mm)
Height: 4–6" (10–15 cm)

Upon initial examination, stairstep moss looks like a solid mat, but upon closer inspection, notice how each individual stem resembles a set of steps, with each one representing a year's growth. Also called splendid feather moss, they have a dainty, feathery appearance even though the moss tends to cover large areas. Each of the tiny branches boasts simple leaves that fan out like tiny ferns. Found in stable, old-growth forests, more often in low to mid elevations, it does not tolerate sunny conditions. If the large trees perish, it will not live long afterward. It also requires fairly high nutrients in a more humus-type soil with consistent moisture. This moss sexually reproduces by spores that are dispersed on the wind, along with asexually by growing out to the side, touching in the soil, and continuing to grow.

CREEPING OREGON GRAPE
Berberis repens
Barberry family (Berberidaceae)
Quick ID: Bright yellow cluster of flowers; leathery leaves with toothed edges; clusters of blue berries
Height: 4–12" (10–30 cm)
Bloom season: April–June

Growing in a variety of woodlands, this short shrub thrives along the forest floor, making it easy to miss unless the brightly colored, yellow flowers are in full bloom or the blue berries are visible among the ground foliage. Sometimes called holly grape due to the similar-looking foliage of the familiar holly leaf, the leaves of the Oregon grape are also evergreen like holly. The foliage changes from deep green to more of an orange or red in the winter, greening again in the spring. The eye-catching yellow flowers are important to bees and other pollinators in the spring, plus bears feed upon the berries during the autumn. White-tailed and mule deer, elk, and bighorn sheep eat the foliage throughout the year. Due to its low-growing nature, creeping Oregon grape is resilient when it comes to fires, and regenerates through rhizomes and seeds.

CREEPING JUNIPER
Juniperus horizontalis
Cypress family (Cupressaceae)
Quick ID: Green-blue; overlapping, short, sharp needles; reddish-brown bark with thin, shredded appearance; blue, berrylike cones
Height: 6–10" (15–25 cm)
Bloom season: April–June

Along the slopes in open meadows and rocky fields, creeping juniper provides important cover and forage for a number of species. This branching evergreen with small, prickly needles will stretch nearly 15' (4.6 m) wide and is a favorite hiding spot for birds and small mammals. They, as well as bears, eat the roughly 0.25" (0.6 cm), berrylike cones, plus mule and white-tailed deer feed on the foliage during the winter and spring. It produces male and female cones on different plants, meaning they are dioecious, with the female ones being the most prominent blue. Although the birds eat and disperse the seeds, they primarily reproduce when a branch touches the ground and sets roots. Found on both sides of the Continental Divide, the pyramidal-shaped Rocky Mountain juniper, *Juniperus scopulorum*, stands nearly 20' (6.1 m) tall and is equally utilized by mammals and birds.

THIMBLEBERRY
Rubus parviflorus
Rose family (Rosaceae)
Quick ID: 4–8" (10–20 cm), 5-lobed leaves; 5-petaled white blossoms; flattish raspberry-like fruit
Height: 19–59" (48–150 cm)
Bloom season: May–July

Prolific along the shaded trails where ferns, stinging nettles, and false hellebore abound, thimbleberries form a lush understory with their large maple-shaped leaves. In the early summer, 1–1.5" (2.5–4 cm) white flowers emerge, eventually ripening to bright red, raspberry-like, fuzzy, 0.4"- to 0.9"-wide (1- to 2-cm-wide) fruit loaded with seeds. The flowers attract a number of pollinators in the spring, and birds and small mammals depend upon the prolific berries. Thimbleberry is also important to bears, who eat the shoots and fruit, providing a food source from the spring to midsummer. The western red raspberry (*Rubus idaeus*) looks similar, with the classic raspberry 5-lobed leaf, white flowers, and red fruit, but the leaves are smaller than the thimbleberries', and raspberries have a more bramble-growing character, with abundant thorns.

GREEN ALDER
Alnus viridis
Birch family (Betulaceae)
Quick ID: Smooth, gray bark; oval leaves with serrated edges and pointed at end; catkins
Height: 6–10" (15–25 cm)
Bloom season: April–May

Growing in dense stands in mid-level elevations along avalanche slopes and open forests, alders pioneer areas where soil nutrients are low, such as near receding glaciers, since their roots are equipped with nitrogen-fixing nodules. These utilize bacteria, capturing atmospheric nitrogen and converting it into a form the plants can use. As these fast-growing shrubs drop leaves, and eventually decompose into the earth when they die, they improve the soil, allowing other species to proliferate. Each shrub has male and female catkins on the same plant. Two 4"-long (5–10-cm-long) male catkins hang in groups of two to four, and the erect, reddish female catkins are a mere 0.5" (1 cm) long. The seeds are sought by pine siskins, chickadees, grouse, and many other birds, while beavers, muskrats, snowshoe hares, and cottontail rabbits consume the bark, twigs, and leaves.

SHRUBBY CINQUEFOIL
Dasiphora fruticosa
Rose family (Rosaceae)
Quick ID: Clusters of 5-petaled, yellow flowers; reddish-brown, shredded-looking bark; 1"-wide (2-cm-wide) palmated leaves
Height: 1–4' (30–122 cm)
Bloom season: June–August

Shrubby cinquefoil, also called potentilla, is a common shrub in home gardens known for its hardy and non-fussy growing requirements. Its wild relative shares the same characteristics. Shrubby cinquefoil thrives from grasslands to mountain meadows, as well as around wetlands, or even in conifer forests. The cheerful, bright yellow flowers are 0.75–1" (2–2.5 cm) wide and continue throughout most of the summer, providing forage for pollinators. The foliage is equally distinct, with 1"-wide (2-cm-wide), slightly fuzzy leaves with three to nine narrow leaflets. Cinquefoil is generally considered a deer-resistant plant in the home garden. The wild version doesn't provide a significant food source for ungulates, but the seeds are used by small mammals and birds. Since it encompasses so much terrain, shrubby cinquefoil is important cover for these small species.

WOODS' ROSE
Rosa woodsii
Rose family (Rosaceae)
Quick ID: Red stems with thorns; 5–9 leaflets on each leaf; 2"-wide (5-cm-wide) light pink, 5-petaled flowers; orange to red rose hips
Height: 2–5' (61–152 cm)
Bloom season: May–June

There are a number of rose varieties in the area, including the prickly rose, *Rosa acicularis*, the official flower of Alberta, but Woods' rose is one of the most common. Woods' roses grow in riparian areas, drier grasslands, and within the understory of open, mixed forests. Blooming in the late spring, the pink flowers, each one only lasting for a day, perfume the area with their sweet fragrance. The shrubs form dense thickets by sending out copious suckers, reducing soil erosion, along with providing exceptional cover for birds and small mammals. Porcupines, beavers, and mule deer eat the leaves, while elk and moose browse the twigs. Rose hips are desired by birds, bears, and small mammals, particularly since they remain on the bushes throughout the winter.

PRICKLY CURRANT
Ribes lacustre
Gooseberry family (Grossulariaceae)
Quick ID: Deeply edged, heart-shaped leaf with 5 to 6 lobes; prickly stems; clusters of pink, saucer-shaped flower with darker center; dark berries
Height: 3–4' (1–1.2 m)
Bloom season: May–June

Well-armed with dense thorns the entire length of the stem, prickly currants' rightly earned name describes its thorny nature. Also called bristly black currant due to its prolific black-colored, berrylike fruit, this native is found in moist and nutrient-rich areas along riparian forests, at the edges of meadows, and in avalanche chutes. Although often present in the understory of open woodlands, as the plants can tolerate some shade, they produce more abundantly in sunnier areas. Deer, elk, and sometimes mountain goats eat the foliage. And while the berries aren't as flavorful as some of the domesticated varieties, they are tasty to bears, birds, and small mammals. All currants, except for specifically developed resistant varieties, are host plants of blister rust, a non-native fungus that infects and often kills 5-needle pine species.

CHOKECHERRY
Prunus virginiana
Rose family (Rosaceae)
Quick ID: Green, glossy, elliptically shaped leaves; clusters of white flowers; deep purple fruit
Height: 6–16' (2–5 m)
Bloom season: May–June

Growing in thickets along the edges of meadows and open areas, choke-cherries are important players in the ecosystem. When they're blooming in the spring, the sweet fragrance of the tiny white flowers fills the air, and butterflies and bees are drawn to the prolific clusters of blossoms. These dense shrubs provide cover and nesting sites for birds. When the berries ripen, beginning at the end of July and continuing until fall, everything from small mammals to grizzlies feasts on the astringent-tasting fruit. Birds flock to the bushes well into the autumn, as the persistent berries provide a good source of late-season forage. Chokecherries are an equally popular fruit for people, harvested outside the parks, with jellies and syrups available in many local shops. Despite the extensive culinary use, chokecherry leaves, stems, and seeds contain hydrocyanic acid, requiring the fruit to be cooked to deactivate the compound before consuming it.

TWINBERRY HONEYSUCKLE
Lonicera involucrata
Honeysuckle family (Caprifoliaceae)
Quick ID: Large, elliptically shaped leaves; twin, tubular yellow flowers; two shiny, black berries between deep reddish-purple bracts
Height: 2–8' (0.6–2 m)
Bloom season: May–July

With attractive light-yellow flowers in the early summer followed by double glossy black berries highlighted by the eye-catching four reddish-purple bracts (scalelike parts of the formation below the petals that are really modified leaves), it's difficult to miss this shrubby honeysuckle at any time of the season. Usually found in moist forests, as well as riparian areas and wetlands, they are fairly common in the mid-level to even higher elevation trails, where there is ample water. The tubular flowers are an important nectar source for butterflies, hummingbirds, and a number of insects in the spring. And while birds such as grosbeaks, waxwings, and ruffed grouse—along with small mammals and even larger ones, like black and grizzly bears—consume the berries that begin ripening toward the end of July, they are considered toxic to humans, particularly children.

SUBALPINE SPIREA
Spiraea splendens var. *splendens*
Rose family (Rosaceae)
Quick ID: Oval-shaped leaves with serrated edges; vibrant dark pink, flat clusters of flowers
Height: 2–3' (61–91 cm)
Bloom season: June–August

Masses of fuzzy-looking deep pink flowers in the higher elevations are a stunning sight. This pink spirea, also commonly called rose meadow-sweet or mountain spirea, looks strikingly similar to popular domestic varieties, and boasts the same attractiveness wrapped in a hardy package. Subalpine spirea thrives in the higher elevations, often around 5,000' (1,524 m), preferring open meadows or slopes in moist areas. The deep green 0.75–2" (2–5 cm) leaves are opposite each other on the stems below each 0.6–2" (1.5–5 cm) cluster of individual flowers that are a mere 0.06–0.08" (1.5–2 mm) in diameter. A favorite of butterflies and other pollinators, its dense brush is cover for birds and small mammals. The white-flowered version, the birch-leaved spirea (*Spiraea betulifolia*), is a common understory shrub.

SILVERBERRY

Elaeagnus commutata
Oleaster family (Elaeagnaceae)
Quick ID: 2"-long (5-cm-long) silvery leaves; yellow, tubular flowers
Height: 3–12' (0.91–4 m)
Bloom season: May–July

In the spring, the sweet, almost citrus-like fragrance of the silverberry is noticed before the beautiful shrubs are seen. Found in mixed prairie habitats, such as around the St. Mary Visitor Center, along with riparian regions and aspen forest edges, silverberry creates attractive and productive groups of shrubs that serve as protection and food for many species. Silverberry is a fast-growing deciduous shrub spread by rhizomes that thrives in disturbed soils. The root nodules fix nitrogen into the soil by capturing atmospheric nitrogen and turning it into a usable form. There are no thorns on silverberries, unlike its non-native relative, the Russian olive (*Elaeagnus angustifolia*). Birds nest among the dense branches and eat the olive-like fruit when it ripens in the fall. Moose frequently browse upon the twigs, and it's a common food source for elk and mule deer.

LEWIS' MOCK ORANGE
Philadelphus lewisii
Hydrangea family (Hydrangeaceae)
Quick ID: Deep green, glossy, oblong leaves; clusters 1–1.5"-wide (2.5–3.8-cm-wide), 4-petaled flowers
Height: 4–8' (1.25–2.5 m)
Bloom season: June–July

Notice the sweetly intoxicating fragrance of the white blossoms along streambanks and wet areas, as well as in grasslands, conifer forests, and on rocky slopes in mid-level elevations, growing best in full sun. The large white, four-petaled flowers cluster in groups of three to eleven at the end of the reddish stems that shed their bark as they age, revealing a gray bark underneath. The deep green leaves are attractive even when the flowers fade. It's no wonder commercial varieties of mock orange are a favorite landscaping choice. Small mammals such as cottontail rabbits eat the foliage, plus deer and elk browse on the twigs during the winter. Squirrels, other rodents, and birds consume the seeds. Mock orange is known to regenerate well after a fire, keeping the soil stable and providing food and habitat to local wildlife.

DEVIL'S CLUB
Oplopanax horridus
Ginseng family (Araliaceae)

Quick ID: Maple leaf–shaped foliage 4–12" (10–30 cm) wide; pyramidal cluster of white flowers followed by bright red berries

Height: 3–6' (1–2 m)
Bloom season: May–July

With enormous leaves and stout stalks, this shrub might seem like a sturdy handhold, but one touch leads to significant regret, as the stems are loaded with stiff, sharp prickles, earning its descriptive common name. Devil's club thrives in wet areas, growing in clumps along stream banks and in the lush undergrowth in the realm of western hemlock, western cedar, and ferns. It is an attractive plant even if it's painful to touch. As a member of the ginseng family, it has equally renowned medicinal uses with antiviral, antifungal, and antibacterial properties. The tiny, white flowers grow in round clusters forming a cone-shaped flower head, ripening into bright red berries. Black bears and grizzlies are impervious to the spiky nature of the plant and routinely feed upon the berries, seeds, and even prickly stems.

COMMON SNOWBERRY
Symphoricarpos albus
Honeysuckle family (Caprifoliaceae)
Quick ID: Small, oval leaves opposite each other on the stem; pinkish-white bell-shaped flower; pure white berries
Height: 2–3' (61–91 cm)
Bloom season: June–August

Found throughout terrain ranging from open meadows to mixed forests, snowberries grow just about everywhere up to the subalpine elevations. Snowberry grows in clumps, and each plant is practically as wide as it is tall. Although not strikingly beautiful, nor fragrant as the mock orange nor loaded with berries like the huckleberry, snowberry is one of those inconspicuous plants that play an important role in the ecosystem. The attractive tubular, pinkish flowers attract bees and other pollinators, but it's the snow-white berries that are a consistent food source for bears, small mammals, and a multitude of birds, especially grouse. Deer and bighorn sheep eat the leaves, which have a higher protein content than many other forage plants in the fall and winter, while moose browse on the twigs at this time of year.

ROCKY MOUNTAIN MAPLE
Acer glabrum
Soapberry family (Sapindaceae)

Quick ID: Brown to gray bark; palmated leaves with 3 to 5 lobes; leaves are green in the summer, turning to a vibrant red in the autumn; yellowish-green flowers; winged seeds

Height: 5–6.5' (1.5–2 m)

Bloom season: May–July

The Rocky Mountain maple typically grows with multiple branches as a large shrub versus the single trunk of a small tree, although occasionally it does take on more of a tree form. They are abundant in the lower to mid-level elevations, and although they thrive near water sources, they are also found on dry slopes. They are more shade-tolerant than some other shrubs, allowing them to thrive in mixed forests. With its multibranched nature, it's a natural nesting area for birds and cover for small mammals. White-tailed deer, moose, and elk eat it. At times, it appears as if the dark green leaves are painted with a brilliant crimson, caused by a practically microscopic type of gall mite, *Eriophyes* spp.

MOUNTAIN HUCKLEBERRY
Vaccinium membranaceum
Heath family (Ericaceae)
Quick ID: Broadly oval or elliptical leaves; small, yellowish-pink blossoms hanging from short flower stalks; reddish to deep purple berries less than 0.5" (1 cm) wide
Height: 1–3' (30–91 cm)
Bloom season: May–June

Huckleberry is royalty in Glacier and Waterton Lakes, where huckleberry pie and huckleberry ice cream are must-try treats. Also known as thin-leaf huckleberry, this prolific shrub is commonly found on slopes within conifer forests from mid-level to nearly subalpine elevations. As much as people love huckleberry desserts, black bears and grizzlies depend upon this abundant calorie source. By the end of the summer their diet consists of between 15 to 50 percent of these sweet fruits before hibernation. From the first berries in July until the end of the season, bears consume up to twenty thousand berries a day, which is why trails are often closed during peak berry periods to allow them to feed in peace.

FOOL'S HUCKLEBERRY
Menziesia ferruginea
Heath family (Ericaceae)
Quick ID: Elliptical leaves; scaly bark on mature branches; clusters of salmon-pink, urn-shaped flowers; brown seed capsules with numerous seeds
Height: 3–6' (91–183 cm)
Bloom season: June–August

Fool's huckleberry grows in many of the same regions as the popular huckleberry, and has a similar appearance, but fool's huckleberry is a taller shrub displaying slightly narrower leaves and has a skunky odor if bruised. Unlike huckleberries, the twigs can be sticky. The bell-like flowers of the fool's huckleberry have a more-salmon hue and tend to hang in clusters. As for berries, the fool's huckleberry does not produce the tasty purple berries, instead forming inedible (to people) brownish seed capsules. Deer and elk feed upon the fool's huckleberry leaves, although it's not on the top of their list if there are tastier options at the time. But chipmunks, deer mice, voles, and birds regularly consume the fruits and seeds. In the fall, the foliage turns a beautiful red-orange, brightening the fall forest.

GROUSE WHORTLEBERRY

Vaccinium scoparium
Heath family (Ericaceae)
Quick ID: 0.6"-long (15-mm-long) elliptical leaves; tiny, white-pinkish flowers; red berries the size of matchheads
Height: 6–8" (15–20 cm)
Bloom season: May–June

Growing just above ankle height along the trails where older lodgepole, spruce, and firs thrive, the diminutive grouse whortleberry lines pathways with its delicate appearance. Thriving in the understory in a variety of soil conditions from mid-level to subalpine elevations, look for them in areas with Oregon grape, arnica, and kinnikinnick. Everything is tiny about grouse whortleberries, including the leaves that resemble huckleberry foliage, the urn-shaped pinkish-white flowers, and the sweet-tart red berries growing to a mere 0.16–0.3" (4–6 mm) wide. Even so, bears strip the bushes of berries, along with spruce grouse, ptarmigan, and other birds that feed upon them. Moose browse on the foliage and twigs in the fall before the small plants are buried in snow. They are susceptible to foot traffic, so be careful to stay on the trail.

KINNIKINNICK
Arctostaphylos uva-ursi
Heath family (Ericaceae)

Quick ID: Sprawling growth habit; reddish stems; evergreen, leathery leaves 0.4–1" (1–3 cm) long, rounded at the end; clusters of pinkish, rounded, bell-shaped flowers; bright red berries

Height: 4–8" (10–20 cm)

Bloom season: May–June

There's a long connection between kinnikinnick and bears. The genus name, *Arctostaphylos*, means "bear grape" in Greek, and it's commonly called bearberry, since the bright red berries are consumed by both black bears and grizzlies, who often feed upon these low-growing shrubs along open slopes in the fall and spring. Grouse and other birds, along with small mammals, eat the berries, since they persist throughout the winter, unlike many other species. Kinnikinnick is easy to spot, sprawling over well-drained, often-rocky areas in the open forest or along banks and slopes, covering the soil and providing shelter for small animals. The leathery leaves are yellowish in the spring, green up during the summer, and turn reddish-purple in the autumn.

SASKATOON SERVICEBERRY
Amelanchier alnifolia
Rose family (Rosaceae)
Quick ID: Oval leaves green to reddish-orange in the fall; 5-petaled white flower clusters; clusters of bluish-purple berrylike fruit
Height: 4–12' (1.2–4 m)
Bloom season: April–June

Also called Juneberries, serviceberries are one of the earliest shrubs to bloom with pure white, fragrant flowers that lead to clusters of edible fruit as early as June in the lower elevations. The berry-looking fruit is a pome with a core like an apple and the appearance of a bluish-purple rose hip. They're sweet but mealy, although this doesn't matter to the wildlife. Be vigilant for black bears and grizzlies when serviceberries are ripe. Birds, especially flocks of cedar waxwings, utilize the berries far past the autumn's first frost. Early in the season, the leaves are soft and silvery green, turning a deeper green in the summer and a beautiful reddish-orange by fall. The foliage and twigs are food sources for deer, elk, moose, mountain goats, and bighorn sheep.

RUSSET BUFFALOBERRY
Shepherdia canadensis
Oleaster family (Elaeagnaceae)
Quick ID: Brown-gray, slightly fuzzy twigs; leathery green leaves; tiny, yellow flowers; oval orange to red berrylike fruit
Height: 6–8' (2–2.5 m)
Bloom season: April–May

Russet buffaloberry is a sturdy shrub with deep green, leathery leaves, sometimes with a silvery-gray tinge, which are rounded on the ends and have rust-colored speckles on the undersides. Bright orange to red berries adorn the bushes by the mid- to late summer. Individual shrubs produce either disk-shaped brownish male or yellow-greenish, funnel-shaped, inconspicuous 4-lobed female flowers. Only the female plants produce fruit. Growing in open wooded areas in lower to mid-level elevations, they provide essential forage and cover for a number of birds and mammals. Deer and elk eat the leaves, and birds and bears consume the berries. While the berries are edible, they aren't particularly tasty due to the presence of saponins, compounds that cause foaming when the berries are crushed with water.

Glacier NPS

AMERICAN ROCKBRAKE
Cryptogramma acrostichoides
Maidenhair Fern family (Pteridaceae)
Quick ID: Two different kinds of frond; dense rhizome mass
Height: 8–12" (20–30 cm)

Like the tenacious brittle bladder fern, the American rockbrake grows in the crevices and rock ledges where just enough soil collects to support their growth. It thrives near small streams, waterfalls, or rock seeps, especially where there is some shade to prevent them from drying out in the hot sun. There are fertile and sterile fronds on all ferns. The fertile fronds create the spores, while the non-fertile ones manage the photosynthesis of the plant. When it comes to the American rockbrake, these different fronds are easy to tell apart. The fertile fronds are 2–10" (5–25 cm) long with 2 sets of leaflets. The sterile ones are 1–8" (3–20 cm) long and have rounder, thicker leaflets instead of the classic feathery fern appearance. Growth is vigorous in the spring, with the leaves dying back in the fall, often accumulating at the crowded base.

STROMATOLITES

Quick ID: Groups of stone resembling circles, swirls, or spirals
Type: Sedimentary

Among the fascinating whorls and striations in the geology of Glacier and Waterton Lakes are the remains of ancient blue-green algae that formed when an enormous inland sea covered the region. These cyanobacteria photosynthesized nutrients while expelling oxygen. They expanded their colonies by capturing the sediments in the water among the slimy mats they formed, ultimately creating layers upon layers of cone- or column-shaped structures that constantly grew toward the sunlight. From today's vantage point, looking at the fossilized remnants of these blue-green algae groups from a different angle, they often appear as swirls, or sometimes like a head of cabbage sliced in half, in the stone. Some still have a cone or rounded shape. While they're found throughout the area, stromatolites are prominent along the Highline Trail, near Grinnell Glacier, and along the Crypt Lake Trail in Waterton Lakes.

ARGILLITE
Quick ID: Reds and green
Type: Sedimentary

It's difficult to miss the beautiful red and green hues of some of Glacier and Waterton Lakes' rocks, whether it's noticeable in bands along the mountainsides, stones in the lakes and rivers, or along a trail. This metamorphosed mudstone is evidence of the long-term effects of water and layers of mud settling over time when the area was an inland sea. There are areas, such as along the Grinnell Glacier Trail, where hikers walk upon the ripples and cracks in the mud of this ancient seabed. The rich, red rocks are the result of oxidized iron within the mudstone. The greens are the same type of stone, but there was less iron available when the rock was formed. They are very visible in St. Mary and Many Glacier, and are the reason Red Rock Canyon in Waterton Lakes and Red Rock Falls and Lake in Glacier have their descriptive names.

QUARTZITE
Quick ID: Grainy texture, sometimes sparkly; white or sometimes pink or reddish
Type: Metamorphic

Not quite as prominent as the striking red and green argillite, the glittering quartzite is quick to catch people's attention. During the process of mountain building, quartz-rich sedimentary stone (typically sandstone) was compressed and changed by heat and pressure to form bands of quartzite between the sedimentary layers. Because of this, it's an extremely hard rock, unlike some of the other types in the area. In many situations, quartzite is more grayish than white, but in certain areas of Glacier and Waterton Lakes it takes on a pink to reddish hue. This is due to the presence of iron, which is no surprise, since it's often found embedded within the red argillite. Notice it in the Red Rock Canyon in Waterton Lakes, as well as along the cliff on the north side of Ptarmigan Tunnel in Glacier.

LIMBER PINE
Pinus flexilis
Pine family (Pinaceae)
Quick ID: Bunches of 5 needles between 1.5–3" (4–8 cm) long; 3–6" (8–15 cm) conical cones; windswept and gnarled
Height: 10–40' (3–12 m)

Visitors in the harsh, arid environment of Glacier and Waterton Lakes' higher elevations can't miss the gnarled forms of living and dead limber pines. Typically growing between 4,000 and 6,230' (1,220–1,900 m), stands of limber pines capture and hold precious moisture critical for other vegetation, and their nutritious seeds provide food for birds and other wildlife. To survive in this difficult terrain, deep taproots hold them fast, and their supple branches withstand the intense winds without breaking. They utilize a complex relationship with the soil fungi to obtain nutrients they can't pull on their own from the sparse soil. These slow-growing trees don't reach maturity until they're at least fifty years old, yet can live more than one thousand years if they are not affected by white pine blister rust or the mountain pine beetle, two issues threatening their existence.

WHITEBARK PINE
Pinus albicaulis
Pine family (Pinaceae)
Quick ID: Groups of 5 needles that are 1–3" (2–6 cm) long; roundish, purple cones 2–3"
(5–8 cm) long; often gnarled, shrublike krummholz
Height: 20–50' (6–15 m)

Growing above 5,500' (1,700 m), the whitebark pine is a critical resource
for a number of species, including the Clark's nutcracker and grizzly bear.
The Clark's nutcracker pulls the large, stonelike seeds out of the cones,
since the cones don't open on their own, stashing tens of thousands of
them throughout a season. Grizzlies naturally take advantage of this high-
calorie food source by digging up some of these caches. What's left is fed
upon by the nutcrackers, as well as squirrels and other small mammals.
The nutcracker is also critical to the regeneration of the whitebark pine,
as it sometimes buries the seeds, offering better chances of germination.
As with the limber pine, efforts to thwart blister rust, as well as the mountain pine beetle, are ongoing within both parks.

WESTERN WHITE PINE
Pinus monticola
Pine family (Pinaceae)
Quick ID: Blue-green needles in bundles of 5; needles are 1.75–4" (4–10 cm) long; gray bark
Height: 100–165' (30–50 m)

The 6–10"-long (15–25-cm-long), slightly curved pinecones are easy to spot along the Camas Road, as well in other areas surrounding Lake McDonald. Like the limber and whitebark pines, the western white pine has bundles, called fascicles, of five needles each. Although it is found at lower elevations than the others, this pine is equally susceptible to the blister rust infection. The western white pine stands out, with a gray trunk that becomes more furrowed and scaly as it matures up to 3' (1 m) in diameter. The needles look wispy from a distance and are soft to the touch, while the branches sweep upward and are more open than many other pines. The cones are a valuable food source for birds and wildlife, and adorn the treetops as they mature in August and September.

81

LODGEPOLE PINE
Pinus contorta
Pine family (Pinaceae)
Quick ID: Groups of 2 yellow-green needles 1.5–3" (4–8 cm) long; tall and straight; brown or grayish bark
Height: 40–115' (12–35 m)

This provincial tree of Alberta makes up many of the forest landscapes, particularly in post–forest fire areas in Glacier and Waterton. The 1–2" (3–6 cm) long, round or oval-shaped female cones tend to be asymmetrical and have a spiny tip on the end of each scale. They grow together, and remain tightly closed for years, yet are viable for over a decade. The cones of the lodgepole pines can be either ordinary or serotinous, the latter requiring the heat of a fire to melt the resinous covering to open the cone and release the seeds. Because lodgepoles germinate in large groups after a fire event, they grow thick and tall, earning the nickname "doghair" stands, as well as the obvious moniker, as these straight trees are used as poles for tepees and other structures.

PONDEROSA PINE

Pinus ponderosa
Pine family (Pinaceae)

Quick ID: Tall with large-diameter trunk; yellow-green 3–10" (7–25 cm) needles in bunches of 3; sturdy, alternating branches start halfway up mature trees; broad top on the tree

Height: 98–164' (30–50 m)

It is perfectly acceptable to smell the bark of this tree on a warm summer day to appreciate its unique vanilla-like fragrance. Often standing well over 100' (30 m) tall and up to 30" (76 cm) in diameter, ponderosa pines are found in mixed coniferous forests or open parks in Glacier, but not in Waterton Lakes. Mature ponderosa pines withstand low-intensity fires by shedding the thick, chunky bark, preventing the heat from damaging the cambium, which is one reason they can live to six hundred years old, although higher-intensity wildfires pose a more-problematic scenario. Birds and squirrels utilize the seeds from the 3–6"-long (8–15-cm-long) cones, and porcupines are known to eat the inner bark and sometimes the limbs of younger trees.

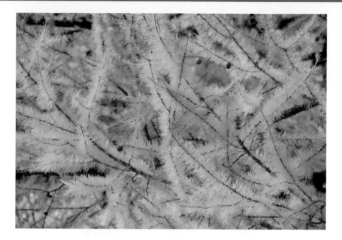

WESTERN LARCH
Larix occidentalis
Pine family (Pinaceae)
Quick ID: Lighter green, soft needles; 1–1.5" (2–4 cm) long with 15 to 30 needles per cluster; turns brilliant yellow-gold in October; cones 1–1.5" (2–4 cm)
Height: 100–200' (30–61 m)

Visitors in the autumn are in awe of the riot of brilliant yellow-gold displays brightening the tree-covered mountains on the west side of the Continental Divide and along US 2 to East Glacier. The display usually peaks around the third week in October. In Waterton Lakes, the subalpine larch (*Larix lyalli*), the dominant larch species, is seen near Upper Rowe Lake. These deciduous conifers lose their chlorophyll in the fall and subsequently shed their needles (leaves), creating a golden pathway for autumn hikers. In the spring, soft bright-green needles emerge. Like other trees in fire-prone regions, larch trees have mechanisms to survive lower-intensity forest fires, such as shedding their lower branches and having thick bark that forms a shield, protecting them from the damaging heat.

DOUGLAS-FIR
Pseudotsuga menziesii
Pine family (Pinaceae)
Quick ID: Thick, horizontally furrowed, gray bark; bluish-green thin needles 1" (2 cm) long form all around stems; soft to the touch
Height: 50–150' (15–46 m)

There are many versions of the Douglas-fir cone fables, most of which involve mice hiding under the cones' scales for safety. Noticing what resembles their tiny hind legs and tails sticking out from beneath the scales is one of the easiest ways to identify this prominent variety growing in forests on both sides of the Continental Divide. They are often found where western hemlocks thrive, along with western oak ferns (*Gymno-carpium dryopteris*) and queencup beadlilies. Even though Douglas-firs have short needles similar to Engelmann spruce, the Douglas-fir needles are flat and softer to the touch. Cones are 2–4" (5–10 cm) long and pointed, with purplish-brown male pollen cones and bright green female ones that hang down from the branches, typically producing a heavy cone crop every five to seven years.

SUBALPINE FIR
Abies lasiocarpa
Pine family (Pinaceae)
Quick ID: Cones grow upward at the top of the tree; bluish-green needles 0.5–1.5" (1–4 cm) long; slender with narrow crown
Height: 65–115' (20–35 m)

At the tree line or above, the tall, slender conifers with short branches and a crown of upward-pointing cones are the unmistakable subalpine firs. Most of the time they rarely grow more than 12" (30 cm) in diameter, especially at the higher elevations in difficult terrain, where their normally stately appearance can take on the stunted and gnarled krummholz characteristic, with much smaller trunks. One of their most distinctive characteristics is the distinct purple or gray cones that stand upright, instead of hang, on the branches, particularly near the top of the tree. The short blue-green needles are somewhat flat and waxy, and tend to flare slightly upward along the stems. When young, the smooth gray bark often has horizontal resin-heavy blisters, and as it matures, it develops a thicker bark with large scales.

WESTERN HEMLOCK
Tsuga heterophylla
Pine family (Pinaceae)
Quick ID: Long and drooping branches; flat 0.25–0.75" (0.6–2 cm) shiny needles are deep green on the top and whitish underneath
Height: 125–175' (38–53 m)

The stately western hemlocks are part of a unique inland rain forest landscape found along the Trail of the Cedars and McDonald Creek. Western hemlocks and western red cedars are both climax species, the trees that ultimately shade and outcompete other species over hundreds of years after the area was first cleared by fire. Although western hemlocks share the same environment and thrive in the deep shade, they have deeply grooved bark in thick, flat ridges instead of the shredded appearance of western red cedar. The small needles, which are uneven in size even when located on the same twig, radiate opposite each other along the stem. Small, 0.75–1" (2–2.5 cm), hanging cones start out a greenish color and mature to light brown in the early fall. These large trees are ideal sites for cavity-nesting birds.

WESTERN RED CEDAR
Thuja plicata
Pine family (Pinaceae)
Quick ID: Flat, fernlike sprays of leaves made up of overlapping scales; fibrous, stringy, reddish-brown bark; enormous tree
Height: 50–195' (15–59 m)

Walking along the Trail of the Cedars, as well as along the John's Lake Trail, feels like stepping back into a primordial rain forest. Researchers believe that many of the trees originated in the early 1500s. This ecosystem among the giants is the realm of long-toed salamanders, woodpeckers, squirrels, mountain lions, and even grizzlies. The massive western red cedars line the boardwalk and are easy to spot, not only because some of them are over 100' (30 m) tall and 10' (3 m) in diameter, but because their stringy, vertically running bark is unlike any other tree in the parks. Their foliage, which is a typical cedar-looking sweeping spray of flat leaves made up of overlapping scales, often has the 0.5" (1 cm) cones growing along the top of the branches instead of hanging below them.

QUAKING ASPEN
Populus tremuloides
Willow family (Salicaceae)
Quick ID: Whitish-green bark furrowed with gray and black marks; heart-shaped, 1.5–3"
(4–8 cm) leaves that are light green in the spring and brilliant gold in the autumn
Height: 16–65' (5–20 m)

The bright spring green leaves welcome early-season visitors, and during the summer, the aspen groves are typically thick with plant life, providing habitat for birds and wildlife. By autumn, their finale is a riot of brilliant yellows and golds before the monochromatic winter. While there might appear to be hundreds of individual trees in an area, aspens are clones on a common root system. Although they reproduce asexually, they produce seeds from the flowers on the catkins that adorn the branches. To better survive in this harsh climate, aspen bark also has the unique ability to produce chlorophyll, and the trees store carbohydrates in the bark for the winter. This rich resource is utilized by deer, moose, and elk that browse upon the twigs and bark during the winter.

GREENE'S MOUNTAIN ASH
Sorbus scopulina
Rose family (Rosaceae)
Quick ID: Shiny, deep green leaves divided into 9 to 13 leaflets; flat clusters of tiny white flowers in the spring; clusters of bright red-orange berries
Height: 3–12' (1–4 m)

The mountain ash trees of Glacier and Waterton Lakes, whether Greene's mountain ash or the shrubbier western mountain ash (*Sorbus sitchensis*), are beautiful and productive. Growing from the valleys to subalpine regions, these large, attractive shrubs bloom with palm-size clusters of white flowers followed by a prolific profusion of bright red-orange berries that persist throughout the winter, making them an important food source for birds and mammals. Propagation typically takes place when birds such as grouse and cedar waxwings eat and disperse the seeds. Autumn hikers will quickly notice an ample supply of both black bear and grizzly scat filled with mountain ash berries, particularly along the Grinnell Glacier Trail, indicating the high use of this late-season crop. Elk, deer, and bighorn sheep browse on the leaves and twigs.

HARLEQUIN DUCK
Histrionicus histrionicus
Duck, Geese, Swan family (Anatidae)

Quick ID: Male—slate-gray body; white cheeks; white stripes and spots outlined in black; chestnut flanks and crown stripes. Female—brown plumage; round head; short, blue-gray bill; 3 white patches on the side of the head.

Length: 14–20" (35–51 cm)
Weight: 17–26 oz (485–750 g)
Wingspan: 22–26" (56–66 cm)

These striking ducks migrate from the West Coast to a handful of fast-moving streams within the region. Bachelor males arrive in April through early May, followed by paired females returning with their lifelong mates that were selected on the coast to the same stream (or river in other areas) drainage in which she was born. They remain close to each other until she finishes laying five to seven eggs in an extremely well-hidden nest. After the final egg is laid, the male returns to the coast, making a second breeding attempt impossible in the case of flooding or other reason for clutch failure. Upper McDonald Creek offers one of the highest concentrations of harlequin ducks in the region; they are also spotted at Cameron Falls in Waterton Lakes.

COMMON GOLDENEYE
Bucephala clangula
Duck, Geese, Swan family (Anatidae)

Quick ID: Male—black/iridescent green head; oval white spot on cheek at base of the bill; white on belly, sides, wings, and tail; golden iris. Female—brown head with gray body; light collar; white on wings; golden iris.

Length: 16–20" (40–51 cm)
Weight: 28–35 oz (800–1,000 g)
Wingspan: 30–33" (76–83 cm)

With large heads and a striking gold-colored iris, the common goldeneye and the Barrow's goldeneye (*Bucephala islandica*) are easy to spot. Telling them apart is a bit more of a challenge, although the common goldeneye male's head is peaked, versus rounded, and has a white oval patch on each cheek, instead of crescent-shaped. Female goldeneyes have a more sloped forehead than their counterparts. Their bill is dark brown, often with yellow on the end. When they're not on lakes or rivers diving for aquatic insects, small fish, or plants, their wings propel them up to 40 mph (64 km/h) over the water.

Jacob W. Frank, Glacier NPS

COMMON MERGANSER

Mergus merganser

Duck, Geese, Swan family (Anatidae)

Quick ID: Male—dark green head; white body; black back; long, reddish-orange bill. Female—shaggy, rust-colored crest on head; light gray body; white on sides and belly; reddish-orange bill.

Length: 21–28" (53–71 cm)

Weight: 32–76 oz (1–2 g)

Wingspan: 34–37" (86–94 cm)

Mergansers seem to play "Now you see them, now you don't" on lakes and rivers. Gliding peacefully along the surface of the water, it only takes a disturbance, or spotting a fish, for them to disappear in a flash under the water. When they're not cruising for a meal, groups of mergansers are found sunning themselves on a log or rock. In the spring, females search out nesting areas near water in the cavities of trees, but also within rock crevices or other protected places, sometimes commandeering other ducks' nests. The female lays six to seventeen eggs, and within one to two days of hatching, the chicks will leave the nest to join their mother on the water.

MALLARD

Anas platyrhynchos

Duck, Geese, Swan family (Anatidae)

Quick ID: Male—iridescent green head with white ring at base; brown-gray body, bright yellow bill; orange feet. Female and nonbreeding male—mottled buff to gray; eye stripe; orange bill; orange feet.

Length: 20–26" (51–66 cm)

Weight: 2–3 lbs (0.9–1.3 kg)

Wingspan: 32–37" (81–94 cm)

These well-known ducks are common residents in many of the lower-elevation waters. Males are easily recognized with the eye-catching iridescent green head and neck, and both sexes have bright blue patches on the upper wing that are visible during flight. Mallards cluster in groups as a protective measure, and even when sleeping, some keep one eye open to watch for potential threats. They feed along the surface or at the edges of the water, and although they don't dive, they are known for tipping upside down with their feet straight up in the air to forage in the shallow water, consuming crayfish, insects, and aquatic plants.

AMERICAN COOT
Fulica americana
Coot family (Rallidae)
Quick ID: Slate-gray plumage; white bill often with a red mark at the top; small tail; reddish eye
Length: 16–17" (41–43 cm)
Weight: 21–25 oz (0.6–0.7 kg)
Wingspan: 23–25" (58–64 cm)

These roundish birds have a body shaped like a chicken and are a vocal bunch with a cacophony of squawks, cackles, and grunts. Primarily herbivores, they forage or dive, feasting on seeds, pondweeds, algae, and occasionally tadpoles, insects, and crayfish. They'll also feed on the land, scurrying back to the water with their quick, waddling walk at any sign of danger. Normally docile characters, coots are aggressive to other birds when defending a nesting site, their floating creation hidden among the reeds. Since they need to run along the top of the water to take flight, coots are more vulnerable to eagles and other birds of prey when the waters freeze and limit their avenues of escape. At times the predators seize the unfortunate coots as they huddle close together in the shrinking open water.

Jacob W. Frank, Glacier NPS

COMMON LOON
Gavia immer
Loon family (Gaviidae)
Quick ID: Black head and neck divided by two broad patches of white with vertical black stripes; black back with white spotted pattern; pointed black bill
Length: 26–36" (66–91 cm)
Weight: 5.5–13 lbs (2.5–5.9 kg)
Wingspan: 3.5–4.5' (1–1.4 m)

The haunting call of a loon across a wilderness lake is a reminder of the importance of these pristine places. Scan the water surface to spot the black head, white necklace with black stripes, and speckled back, although sometimes their body sits low in the water to make them more inconspicuous. Loons are not ducks, and are powerful swimmers and divers, performing extraordinarily fast and impressive maneuvers below the surface in their pursuit of fish. Being seasonally monogamous, they may pair up for many years, but will switch partners if necessary. After a courtship period, they build a nest of plant materials near the water's edge where the female lays one to two eggs. Both parents care for the chicks, including giving them piggyback rides.

BUFFLEHEAD
Bucephala albeola
Duck, Geese, Swan family (Anatidae)
Quick ID: Male—dark, iridescent head with large, pie-wedge white patch on the back.
Female—buff coloration on the top, white on the bottom; white patch on cheek.
Length: 13–16" (33–41 cm)
Weight: 10–22 oz (283–624 g)
Wingspan: 17–22" (43–56 cm)

With large, rounded heads, bufflehead males are easy to identify. When the light catches it right, the dark head shimmers in a beautiful purple and green iridescence. Buffleheads are exceptional swimmers, feeding upon aquatic invertebrates, snails, dragonfly larvae, and zooplankton. They quickly plunge beneath the water, often popping to the surface like a feathery bobber. Buffleheads nest in cavities, but not ones they create, instead preferring those of northern flickers that are small enough in diameter to discourage goldeneyes and mergansers. During the summer, females scope out potential nest cavities for the next season. Although they are territorial during the breeding season, after it's over, they gather in small groups on many of the frontcountry lakes.

TUNDRA SWAN
Cygnus columbianus
Duck, Geese, Swan family (Anatidae)
Quick ID: Pure white; black bill with yellow spot at base; black legs and feet
Length: 42–58" (107–147 cm)
Weight: 8–23 lbs (3.6–10 kg)
Wingspan: 65–79" (1.65–2 m)

Tundra swans fly through the area on their migration to and from their breeding grounds on the tundra and the temperate coastal areas where they spend the winters. Flying overhead in a V formation, their distinct higher-pitched *ou-ho* calls are heard from a distance. Although they look similar to trumpeter swans, tundra swans are smaller and have a distinct yellow spot on their more-concave bill, where the trumpeter's bill is completely dark. The trumpeter's call is also deeper. Tundra swans are large birds, yet sometimes feed like dabbling ducks, with their hind ends and feet in the air as they reach nearly a yard (1 m) below the surface to snag tubers and aquatic vegetation. They mate for life and stay together throughout the year.

CANADA GOOSE
Branta canadensis
Duck, Geese, Swan family (Anatidae)
Quick ID: Black head and neck; white cheek and under the chin; buff body
Length: 30–43" (0.75–1.1 m)
Weight: 6.5–20 lbs (3–9 kg)
Wingspan: 50–67" (1.25–1.7 m)

These highly adaptable waterfowl are a common sight throughout North America, and reside on the lakes and rivers in both parks, excluding the alpine regions. They are known migrators, yet some stay throughout the winter. Primarily herbivores, they graze on fresh vegetation on the land as well as aquatic plants by either skimming along the surface or plunging their head under the water with their tails sticking straight up. Canada geese begin breeding at three years old and pair up for life. The female is tasked with building the nest. After they hatch, the goslings feed themselves within a couple of days, but the parents will aggressively hiss and even bite if a threat is too close. They are well-known for their honking vocalizations, and can be extremely noisy in large flocks.

SPOTTED SANDPIPER
Actitis macularius
Sandpiper family (Scolopacidae)
Quick ID: Brown back; speckled breast; orange bill
Length: 7–8" (18–20 cm)
Weight: 1–2 oz (28–57 g)
Wingspan: 14.5–16" (37–41 cm)

Spotted sandpipers aren't particularly showy, but their jerking, bobbing motion as they walk, as well as their very loud series of high-pitched *weets*, is a giveaway. Look for these medium-size brown and spectacled shorebirds along lakes, rivers, and streams rimmed with vegetation. They are primarily solitary birds, but during the breeding season traditional roles are reversed as the slightly larger female stakes out and defends her preferred nesting area. The female is the one who attracts the mate. She pairs up with a male, sets a clutch, then finds a new mate, laying up to four nests per season. After her work is done, the individual males incubate each clutch and care for the chicks. They are found on all the major lakes in Glacier, as well as Lower Waterton Lake, Linnet Lake, the Maskinonge, and Cameron Lake in Waterton Lakes.

RING-BILLED GULL
Larus delawarensis
Gull family (Laridae)
Quick ID: Light gray back; white on head and breast; dull yellow bill with black ring on the end
Length: 19–21" (48–53 cm)
Weight: 15–37 oz (0.4–1 kg)
Wingspan: 49–51" (1.2–1.3 m)

Visitors to Glacier and Waterton Lakes are often surprised to see this normally beach-dwelling bird soaring among the mountain vistas, or begging for food in areas where people gather. But there are a number of gulls that spend time in both of the parks as they travel from the West Coast to their breeding grounds farther north in Canada. Gulls are not shy, and raucous groups will often hone in on a food source, whether it's unhealthy human snacks or their natural diet of insects, fish, eggs, or even young birds from nests. The ring-billed gull is similar in appearance to the California gull (*Larus californicus*), but the ring-billed gull is smaller and has the distinct black ring around the end of its bill.

AMERICAN WHITE PELICAN
Pelecanus erythrorhynchos
Pelican family (Pelecanidae)
Quick ID: White; black flight feathers; huge orange bill with pouch on the bottom; orange legs
Length: 50–65" (127–165 cm)
Weight: 10–20 lbs (4.5–9 kg)
Wingspan: 8–9' (2.4–2.7 m)

Yes, that's a pelican. Normally viewed as an ocean-dwelling bird, American white pelicans migrate from their coastal wintering grounds into Montana and Alberta, along with other prairie states and provinces. Although they are not abundant, they are sometimes seen in the Upper and Middle Waterton Lakes, as well as St. Mary and Lower St. Mary Lakes in Glacier. American white pelicans primarily eat fish by skimming the surface of the water with their massive bill, scooping up the minnows and fish up to 20" (51 cm) long into their mouths. They'll also eat crawfish, tadpoles, and salamanders from shallow areas. White pelicans are impressive birds with wingspans longer than even a golden eagle's, and are easy to spot flying in a synchronized V formation.

AMERICAN DIPPER
Cinclus mexicanus
Dipper family (Cinclidae)
Quick ID: Dark gray; dark eye with white eyelid; stocky, rounded body
Length: 6–8" (15–20 cm)
Weight: 2–3 oz (57–85 g)
Wingspan: 9–10" (23–25 cm)

These delightful birds make their fast-paced living along the edges of fast-running streams, rivers, and lakes. Their sleek gray plumage blends into rocks, yet they're easy to spot, bobbing on rocks near the swift water before quickly diving in to retrieve small fish, mosquitoes, aquatic insects, or insect larvae. They'll even move rocks at the bottom of the stream to grab a meal. To help them find food, they have a special membrane over their eyes allowing them to see underwater, and their white regular eyelid is often visible when they blink. Dippers are strong underwater swimmers, and are well-insulated with a layer of down covered by well-oiled feathers, allowing them to dive into the freezing water even in subzero (below -17 degrees C) winter temperatures.

randimal / iStock / Getty Images Plus

BALD EAGLE
Haliaeetus leucocephalus
Eagle, Hawk family (Accipitridae)
Quick ID: White head and tail in adults; dark body; hooked, yellow bill; yellow legs with large, visible black talons
Length: 28–38" (71–97 cm)
Weight: 6.5–14 lbs (3–6.3 kg)
Wingspan: 6–7' (1.8–2.1 m)

Adult bald eagles are easy to identify, even from a distance, with their telltale white head and large, white tail as they soar above the landscape, but the juvenile bald eagles throw a wrench into simple identification. Until they are three years old, bald eagles appear brown and mottled, sometimes looking similar to a golden eagle. As they mature, the white feathers on their head progressively fill in until they reach full adulthood around age five. Bald eagles build enormous stick nests high in trees where the female lays two eggs, with the chicks tended by both parents. Once hatched, the parents feed the eaglets fish and small prey until they leave the nest at ten to twelve weeks old. Eagles hunt for fish, ducks, and small mammals, but won't pass up carrion.

Glacier NPS

GOLDEN EAGLE
Aquila chrysaetos
Eagle, Hawk family (Accipitridae)
Quick ID: Golden-brown feathers on head and neck; dark feathers on the rest of the body; dark, hooked bill; feathers go to the feet
Length: 33–38" (84–97 cm)
Weight: 6.5–13.5 lbs (3–6 kg)
Wingspan: 6–7.5' (1.8–2.3 m)

Golden eagles soar above the prairies and among the mountaintops with the long, primary feathers at the end of their wings opening like fingers. Small mammals, birds, and deer are potential prey as they dive at a dizzying 150 mph (241 km/h) to snatch them, often unaware until it's too late. They'll also drag or drive young mountain goats off a cliff given the opportunity. There is sometimes confusion between golden eagles and immature bald eagles, but golden eagles don't have the mottled, piebald appearance of the juveniles, and the feathers of the golden eagle cover the entire length of their leg. Golden eagles migrate to warmer regions in the fall, with the Lake McDonald area being one of the best places to observe the regal birds on their long journey from September to November.

Jacob W. Frank, Glacier NPS

OSPREY
Pandion haliaetus
Osprey family (Pandionidae)
Quick ID: Brown body; light belly and legs; white head with brown band like a mask over the eyes; dark, hooked beak
Length: 21–23" (51–58 cm)
Weight: 3–4.5 lbs (1.3–2 m)
Wingspan: 5–6' (1.5–1.8 m)

These efficient, flying hunters cruise over lakes and rivers, hovering once their prey is spotted, then diving up to 30 mph (48 km/h), sometimes submerging their entire body in the water as they seize a 4–12" (10–30 cm) fish with their talons. At times, bald eagles try to steal their hard-won quarry, resulting in midair acrobatics. Looking a little like a bald eagle, with white on their head, osprey are smaller and fly differently, with steady, deep wingbeats versus an eagle's tendency to glide. Ospreys build large stick nests on the tops of trees (or power poles) near lakes or rivers, and usually reuse the same one each year. The female lays two to four eggs, and she tends to the chicks while the male brings the family food.

GREAT HORNED OWL
Bubo virginianus
Owl family (Strigidae)
Quick ID: Gray-brown; brown face, yellow eyes, large feathered tufts on head
Length: 18–29" (46–74 cm)
Weight: 2–5.5 lbs (0.9–2.5 kg)
Wingspan: 3–4.8' (0.9–1.5 m)

These silent, nighttime hunters are spotted in the open areas of trees or other vantage points where they perch to locate their prey. Turning their head nearly 180 degrees in either direction, they use their exceptional hearing to precisely tune into the sound of prey under the snow or grass. Once detected, the owl quickly flies directly at the oblivious quarry, shifting to a feetfirst approach before grasping it with its strong talons. With a grip of 29 pounds (13 kg) of force, there's not much hope of escape. They frequently decapitate their meal before swallowing the smaller animals whole or tearing larger ones into pieces. Since they cannot digest the hair, bones, teeth, and feathers, they regurgitate the compressed remnants, called pellets, approximately ten hours after consuming it.

Glacier NPS

RED-TAILED HAWK
Buteo jamaicensis
Eagle, Hawk family (Accipitridae)
Quick ID: Brown on the head, back, and sides, sometimes mottled with light feathers; short, flared, reddish tail
Length: 18–26" (46–66 cm)
Weight: 24–52 oz (0.7–1.5 kg)
Wingspan: 3.5–4.5' (1–1.4 m)

Most people are familiar with the ubiquitous, raspy cry of the red-tailed hawk, used for practically any raptor on a television program or movie, along with the signature red tail feathers on some individuals. But red-tailed hawks have a wide variety of color variations, including a rust-colored underbelly or dark feathers on their body. The tail comes in shades of pale to dark cinnamon. When perched, the wings do not extend all the way to the end of the tail, and they soar with occasional slow wingbeats before swooping down to seize a small mammal, or steal a meal from another raptor. Red-tailed hawks usually maintain their pair bond throughout their lives, and use the same nest for subsequent years.

RED-WINGED BLACKBIRD
Agelaius phoeniceus
Blackbird family (Icteridae)
Quick ID: Male—black body; patch of red rimmed with yellow at the bottom on the shoulder. Female—stocky body; brown patterned coloration; light eyebrow.
Length: 7–9" (8–23 cm)
Weight: 1–3 oz (28–85 g)
Wingspan: 12–16" (30–41 cm)

Residents of wetlands on both sides of the Continental Divide, the highly conspicuous males flare their feathers while perched on top of reeds or nearby shrubs, sounding trilling calls and whistles to stake out their territory. Females are far more elusive, hiding among the bulrushes. She builds the 4–7" (10–18 cm) well-hidden nest among the thick vegetation, and both parents tend the chicks for a couple of weeks after hatching. Red-winged blackbirds primarily forage on the ground or along the shore for insects, including grasshoppers, and snails, followed by seeds and berries later in the season. After raising the young, they group with other blackbirds and starlings before migrating south for the winter.

YELLOW-HEADED BLACKBIRD
Xanthocephalus xanthocephalus
Blackbird family (Icteridae)

Quick ID: Male—bright yellow on the head and shoulders; black body; narrow white stripe on wing. Female—less yellow on head; brown feathers; white on wing.

Length: 8–10" (20–25 cm)
Weight: 2–4 oz (57–113 cm)
Wingspan: 16–17" (41–43 cm)

Not quite as abundant as the red-winged blackbird, yellow-headed blackbirds are easy to spot, with nearly the entire top half of their body sporting brilliant yellow plumage. Males have a specific territory with up to eight females in their group, and they defend their area with loud buzzing calls. Each female will build her nest averaging 5–6" (13–15 cm) across and just as deep, where she lays three to five eggs. Both parents take care of the chicks until they venture out of the nest at roughly twelve days old. Like red-winged blackbirds, yellow-headed blackbirds focus on insects during the first part of the summer, switching to seeds as they ripen.

Jacob W. Frank, Glacier NPS

RAVEN
Corvus corax
Crow family (Corvidae)
Quick ID: Completely black; strong, black beak; tail has diamond-shaped outline
Length: 22–27" (56–69 cm)
Weight: 24–57 oz (0.7–1.6 kg)
Wingspan: 45–47" (114–119 cm)

Highly adaptable and resourceful, ravens enjoy a mythical status in cultures throughout the world. Besides using their superior intelligence to secure a meal, they develop long-term pair bonds, sometimes touching wingtips while flying or preening each other during courtship. Ravens and American crows (*Corvus brachyrhynchos*) share much of the same territory in the region, and although they look similar, there are a few distinct differences. Ravens are not as social as crows, and are usually found in pairs instead of larger groups after the young are raised. They are larger, and their tail is diamond-shaped, while the crow's tail looks more rounded or even squared off when in flight. Their vocalizations are easily distinguished, as the raven has a throaty croak, while the crow gives a distinct *caw* to announce its presence.

BLACK-BILLED MAGPIE
Pica hudsonia
Crow family (Corvidae)
Quick ID: Black bill and beak; black head; white underbelly; iridescent blue on the wings and tail
Length: 18–27" (46–69 cm)
Weight: 5–8 oz (142–227 g)
Wingspan: 22–24" (56–61 cm)

Vociferous and entertaining, magpies are beautiful scavengers who share their loud opinions while waiting at a carcass for an opportunity to grab a bite. They also feed upon insects and ticks, plus the eggs and chicks of other birds. Berries and seeds are on the menu later in the season, and they're found practically anywhere there is a consistent food source. These very vocal birds communicate with a wide array of calls, squawks, and shrieks, and perch in the high branches of trees and shrubs. Magpies build large, jumbled stick nests that are roughly 30" (76 cm) in diameter and 20" (51 cm) tall in the middle of sturdy shrubs or small trees, where they raise six to seven nestlings and tend to remain in family groups.

RUFFED GROUSE
Bonasa umbellus
Grouse, Partridge family (Phasianidae)
Quick ID: Light brown, white, and black mottled pattern; crest on head; black band near tip of tail
Length: 16–20" (41–51 cm)
Weight: 16–27 oz (454–765 g)
Wingspan: 20–26" (51–66 cm)

Early in the season, visitors may hear a rhythmic thumping that starts slowly and increases to a rapid, low-frequency flutter resonating throughout the forest. With the black fluff flared around their neck and their whole body puffed up to show off, the males perform this unique display while standing on a fallen tree or a rock. Nests are a well-camouflaged depression at the base of a tree or underneath a shrub where the female incubates and hatches the nine to fourteen eggs. Ruffed grouse prefer mixed forests since they feed on the tips of aspens and willows, as well as herbaceous plants and berries. They gravitate toward trails and roadsides, gathering gravel to fill their gizzard for digestion, and will flush if a threat is too close, startling many hikers.

PamWalker68 / iStock / Getty Images Plus

WHITE-TAILED PTARMIGAN

Lagopus leucura

Grouse, Partridge family (Phasianidae)

Quick ID: Male—grayish-brown overall; white on belly; red mark above eye during breeding season. Female—brown with yellowish tint, black and heavily patterned; both white in the winter and have feathered feet.

Length: 11.5–12.5" (29–32 cm)

Weight: 11.5–17 oz (326–482 g)

Wingspan: 20–22" (51–53 cm)

Typically found above the timberline, ptarmigans are naturally difficult to spot with their exceptional seasonal camouflage, and are sometimes heard before they're seen, clucking in the deep brush along the trail. They turn pure white in the winter to blend in with their monochromatic surroundings, then change back to the patterns of summer to protect them from golden eagles and other predators. When the chicks hatch in mid- to late July, they stay with the mother and family group for eight to ten weeks before dispersing. The young eat insects for a few weeks before switching to the primarily vegetarian diet of willow twigs and leaves, followed by conifer buds during the winter.

Glacier NPS

AMERICAN THREE-TOED WOODPECKER
Picoides dorsalis
Woodpecker family (Picidae)

Quick ID: Male—black with white barring from head to tail; white stripe behind the eye; small yellow cap. Female—black with white on throat and patches underneath; white streaks on cheeks; no yellow cap.

Length: 6.5–8" (17–20 cm)
Weight: 1.6–2.3 oz (46–66 g)
Wingspan: 43–51" (108–129 mm)

The American three-toed woodpecker might not be the showiest woodpecker, with primarily black-and-white coloration, but it's interesting to watch as these industrious birds cling to the trunks of trees looking for the larvae of bark beetles and other insects. At times, they'll stop for a moment, listening for the faintest indication of a tasty meal before either flaking off the bark or pecking vigorously at the targeted spot. They thrive in post-burn areas with dead or dying trees, but are difficult to spot, so it's often more effective to listen for their pecking on the tree, as well as their high-pitched *pik* or rattle-like calls.

alukich / iStock / Getty Images Plus

NORTHERN FLICKER
Colaptes auratus
Woodpecker family (Picidae)

Quick ID: Male—brownish-gray; black spots on belly; yellow/orange underparts of wings and tail; red patch on cheek; black crescent marking on chest. Female—more evenly brown; no red on cheek.

Length: 11–12" (28–31 cm)
Weight: 4–5.5 oz (128–142 g)
Wingspan: 16.5–20" (42–51 cm)

Northern flickers are highly adaptable and commonly seen in meadows, near wetlands, in forests as high up as the tree line, and in burned areas. Unlike other woodpeckers, flickers more often forage on the ground, hopping from one area to the next in search of ants and beetles, which they dig out of the soil instead of drilling them out of a tree trunk. During the latter part of the season, berries and seeds are on the menu. Flickers prefer to nest in aspens or cottonwoods since it's easier to excavate their 3"-wide (8-cm-wide) and 13–16"-deep (33–41-cm-deep) nests in those types of wood, along with reusing nests from other birds.

CEDAR WAXWING
Bombycilla cedrorum
Waxwing family (Bombycillidae)
Quick ID: Gray body; light brown head merges into dusty lemon on breast and body; black mask
Length: 5–7" (14–17 cm)
Weight: 0.9–1.2 oz (26–32 g)
Wingspan: 9–12" (22–30 cm)

Look for this sleek, beautiful bird whenever there's a chirping, trilling party in the shrubs, particularly when berries persist later in the season. Cedar waxwings prefer open forests, as well as the edges between trees and meadows. In the early part of the season, they focus on insects, which are frequently found among willows and less-dense areas near water. But as the berries ripen, these industrious flocks travel from bush to bush busily picking off the fruit, making a production of the endeavor. A couple of unique features are the distinct black mask around the eyes and the bright yellow band at the end of the gray tail. Sometimes there are red tips, which are waxy secretions, toward the end of the wings, but they're not always visible.

Glacier NPS

BROWN CREEPER
Certhia americana
Songbird family (Certhiidae)
Quick ID: Slender, downcurved bill; brown with streaking; white belly; reddish underneath at base of tail
Length: 4.5–5.5" (11–14 cm)
Weight: 0.2–0.3 oz (6–9g)
Wingspan: 6.5–8" (17–20 cm)

A glimpse of motion is usually the first giveaway of the tiny brown creeper as it works the cracks and crevices along the bark of a tree. They gravitate toward mature, mixed forests from lower elevations to subalpine stands. Flying to the base of a tree, the brown creeper plants its feet on either side of its body, grasping the bark with sharp claws and working its way up the trunk, picking at insects along the way. Their brown hues and white streaking provide near invisibility as they flatten themselves against the tree when danger threatens. Nuthatches, such as the red-breasted nuthatch (*Sitta canadensis*), also hunt among the tree bark, but they are larger and gray in color, plus they work their way down the trunks while the brown creepers always move upward.

Glacier NPS

MOUNTAIN CHICKADEE
Poecile gambeli
Chickadee family (Paridae)

Quick ID: Gray body with lighter belly; black cap and bib; white stripe on head; white on cheeks and around head: white stripe on head

Length: 4.5–6" (11–15 cm)
Weight: 0.3–0.5 oz (9–14 g)
Wingspan: 6–8" (15–20 cm)

The mountain and black-capped (*Poecile atricapillus*) chickadees are the prominent species in the parks, and while they are similar in appearance, the easiest way to tell them apart is the mountain chickadee has a white stripe over its eye instead of the solid black cap. Black-capped chickadees are also more likely found in aspen and deciduous forests, while mountain chickadees reside among the conifers. Mountain chickadees have a slightly raspy *chicka-zee-zee-zee* call when danger is close, and their early-season mating song, *fee-bee-bee*, is sung in lower notes than the higher *fee-bee* of the black-capped chickadee. Both are primarily insect eaters, yet they rely on seeds, including those of pines, to survive during the winter.

CLIFF SWALLOW
Petrochelidon pyrrhonota
Swallow family (Hirundinidae)
Quick ID: Upper area metallic blue-black, sometimes greenish; rust on cheeks; white or cream on forehead, chest, and belly
Length: 5–6" (13–15 cm)
Weight: 0.7–1.2 oz (19–34 g)
Wingspan: 11–12" (28–30 cm)

Cliff swallows construct colonies of mud nests on banks of lakes, rivers, and cliff edges by gathering mud in their bills and forming it into pellets. They construct the jug-shaped homes by fashioning a mud ledge onto the surface, then building upon the base before ending with the short entrance tunnel that is 2" (5 cm) wide. But it's not all peace at the colony, as birds sometimes fight over nesting sites, and even steal wet mud from a neighboring nest when the pair is away gathering more materials. They feed mostly on flying insects, and it's an impressive sight to observe a colony taking advantage of an insect swarm. Despite their speed and flying abilities, cliff swallows are prey for everything from hawks to mink.

WHITE-CROWNED SPARROW
Zonotrichia leucophrys
Sparrow family (Emberizidae)
Quick ID: Black-and-white head with white streak down the crown; gray overall with brown on wings and tail; lighter belly; long tail; pale yellow bill
Length: 6–6.5" (15–17 cm)
Weight: 0.9–1 oz (26–28 g)
Wingspan: 8–9.5" (20–24 cm)

Another member of the large sparrow family, white-crowned sparrows are abundant in wetlands, forested edges with brushy habitat, and even in campgrounds. These tiny omnivores hop on the ground and in the shrubs feeding upon insects, or ripened seeds and berries later in the year. With their wide variety of vocalizations, researchers have discovered there is actually a particular dialect of certain regions found within these songs. Some birds are reportedly bilingual, understanding and repeating the calls of sparrows in a neighboring area. White-crowned sparrows bond early in the spring, with the female building the nest as soon as the melting snow allows. By the end of the season they separate, but typically rejoin the following season.

Glacier NPS

DARK-EYED JUNCO
Junco hyemalis
Sparrow family (Emberizidae)
Quick ID: Dark gray overall; black mask; light-colored short, strong bill; long tail
Length: 5.5–6.5" (14–17 cm)
Weight: 0.6–1 oz (17–28 g)
Wingspan: 7–10" (18–25 cm)

Dark-eyed juncos thrive in a wide range of habitats and elevations, even as high as Logan Pass or along the Carthew-Alderson Trail in Waterton Lakes. During the summer, they take advantage of the abundance of insects, hopping along the ground to pick up beetles, caterpillars, and spiders, although they're equally excellent at zipping through thick brush to seize them on the fly. Throughout the rest of the year most of their diet consists of seeds from herbaceous plants and shrubs. Dark-eyed juncos are social birds, grouping together except for a short time when males and females pair up to raise their young before forming flocks once again. Prey for weasels and martens, as well as raptors, they quickly dash into the dense thickets to escape danger.

Jacob W. Frank, Glacier NPS

WESTERN TANAGER
Piranga ludoviciana
Cardinal family (Cardinalidae)

Quick ID: Male—brilliant orange head; bright yellow on neck and chest; black wings with yellow or white bars. Female—drab yellow on head and body; brown wings with pale yellow bars.

Length: 6–7.5" (15–19 cm)
Weight: 0.8–1.5 oz (23–43 g)
Wingspan: 11–12" (28–30 cm)

It's difficult to miss this vibrant resident of conifer and mixed decidu-ous forests. While they're well-known fruit eaters, western tanagers consume numerous insects during the breeding season, when protein requirements are crucial. They often perch high in the shrubs, absolutely motionless as they intently search for insect movement, seizing them off the leaves or snagging them in midair. They'll even take advantage of the sweet treat of flower nectar when they pick insects off the flowers. During the rest of the year, they focus on berries for their primary food sources. When paired, the female builds the nest, and the male brings her food as she incubates the clutch.

BROWN-HEADED COWBIRD
Molothrus ater
Blackbird family (Icteridae)
Quick ID: Male—glossy black; brown head; small, conical dark bill. Female—smaller than male; brown coloration.
Length: 7.5–9" (19–23 cm)
Weight: 1.3–1.8 oz (37–51 g)
Wingspan: 12–15" (30–38 cm)

Found in grasslands and along the forest edges, these native birds have long been associated with large animals such as bison, feeding upon the insects kicked up by the enormous herds of moving animals. With the bison gone, brown-headed cowbirds are best known as a brood parasite that does not build their own nests, but instead lays their eggs in other clutches. Female cowbirds can lay an egg every day for several weeks, sometimes surpassing three dozen each season. Some larger host birds roll out the foreign eggs, while other resourceful ones build a new nest on top of them. Yet, very often the host parents raise the much larger, and much hungrier, cowbird young that demand more attention and food, to the detriment of their own brood.

STELLER'S JAY
Cyanocitta stelleri
Crow family (Corvidae)
Quick ID: Black to dark gray head with crest; iridescent, blue body; long, black bill; long tail
Length: 12–13" (30–33 cm)
Weight: 3.5–5 oz (99–142 g)
Wingspan: 18–19" (45–48 cm)

Colorful, large, and boisterous, it's practically impossible to miss these beautiful birds residing in coniferous and mixed forests. In typical jay fashion, they often make a harsh, loud *shook, shook, shook* call, along with myriad quieter songs. Steller's jays are opportunistic feeders, eating everything from insects, berries, seeds (including those of pines), eggs, and even the nestlings of other birds. At times they might beg at campgrounds or along the trail, but do not give in to their pleas. With their keen corvid (members of the raven and crow family) mind, Steller's jays store extra food in caches in the bark of trees or in small, often self-dug, holes in the ground to utilize them during the winter, and routinely raid the ones left by Clark's nutcrackers.

CANADA JAY
Perisoreus canadensis
Crow family (Corvidae)
Quick ID: Overall gray with dark gray on wings and tail and lighter underneath; white head; black on cap and has a mask to the eyes; short bill; long tail
Length: 10–11" (25–28 cm)
Weight: 2–3 oz (57–85 g)
Wingspan: 17–19" (43–48 cm)

Living in areas ranging from forests to subalpine regions in the summer, Canada jays look similar to Clark's nutcrackers, but Clark's nutcrackers have much longer, pointier bills, are more evenly gray, and have black wings with white underneath. Commonly called camp robbers, Canada jays don't have much fear when it comes to a free meal. They'll steal if they're not watched. As a rule, nearly anything is on the menu, including seeds and berries, insects and spiders, baby birds, carrion, and fungi. Like some others in the crow family, they store their food, but Canada jays first mold it with their saliva to tuck it beneath the tree bark or in a crevice for later use.

CLARK'S NUTCRACKER
Nucifraga columbiana
Crow family (Corvidae)
Quick ID: Light gray; black wings; long, pointed dark bill
Length: 10.5–12" (27–30 cm)
Weight: 4–6 oz (113–170 g)
Wingspan: 17–19" (43–48 cm)

Clark's nutcrackers reside in the higher elevations, and the raucous vocalizations of family groups are unmistakable. They have a long-standing relationship to the 5-needle pines, particularly the whitebark pine, as their bills are well-adapted to breaking open the cones to pry out the seeds. They stash up to tens of thousands of seeds each season, typically carrying as many as ninety at a time, either tucking them behind bark, near rocks, among roots, or in shallow trenches they dig with their bills. What they don't eat can potentially germinate. Beyond the whitebark pine, Clark's nutcrackers have a penchant for ponderosa pine and limber pine seeds, along with insects, amphibians, and small mammals. Because of these high-energy food sources, they nest in the winter, feeding their young the seeds from last season's caches.

KILLDEER
Charadrius vociferus
Plover family (Charadriidae)

Quick ID: Light brown on top and white on chest and belly; 2 black bands along chest; white and black bands on face; orange-reddish iris; long legs

Length: 8–11" (20–28 cm)
Weight: 2.5–4.5 oz (71–128 g)
Wingspan: 18–19" (46–48 cm)

Killdeer might look like other shorebirds, but they are just as easily seen away from the water in open areas of short grass and gravel, including parking areas or trails. They are quick, whether on land or in flight, and are often heard before they are seen with their high, trilling repetitive *dee, dee, dee* cry. Any potential threat in the area elicits an elaborately feigned injury display leading danger away from the ground-level, yet well-camouflaged, nest. The earth-toned and speckled eggs blend in to the area around them, and both parents care for the young. Killdeer feed upon a wide variety of insects and, depending on their location, may include centipedes, snails, and crayfish.

randimal / iStock / Getty Images Plus

WESTERN MEADOWLARK
Sturnella neglecta
Blackbird family (Icteridae)

Quick ID: Heavily patterned brown and white on the top; yellow on chest and belly, with distinct black V band across chest; sharp, pointed bill

Length: 6–10" (15–25 cm)
Weight: 3–4 oz (85–113 g)
Wingspan: 13.5–17" (34–43 cm)

The melodious song of the western meadowlark is the true herald of spring. In March and April, the whistling and warbling songs of the males resound through the grasslands as they perch on rocks, shrubs, or in surrounding trees. They are more likely spotted east of the Continental Divide, but are sometimes seen around Bowman Lake or Big Prairie in the North Fork area of Glacier, as well as throughout the lower elevations in Waterton Lakes. Meadowlarks are ground feeders, using their long bill to work the soil looking for caterpillars, beetles, and other insects. As the summer progresses, they consume seeds from herbaceous plants. Their nest is made of native grasses, sometimes with overhead protection as part of the design.

Glacier NPS

MOUNTAIN BLUEBIRD
Sialia currucoides
Thrush family (Turdidae)

Quick ID: Male—brilliant sky blue; lighter underneath; black tips on wings. Female—drabber brownish-blue; light blue on tail and wing feathers.

Length: 6–8" (15–20 cm)
Weight: 0.95–1.1 oz (27–33 g)
Wingspan: 11–14" (28–36 cm)

Found in open areas usually on the edges of forests, such as near the Bison Paddock and along the Hay Barn area in Waterton Lakes, or at Two Dog Flats near St. Mary, these brilliant birds are seen throughout the parks. Mountain bluebirds nest in a knothole of a tree or in a previous nest created by another cavity-nesting bird. The male scopes out the potential sites, then shows them off to the female by singing while perched near or on the site. The female makes the final decision, and pairs frequently use the same location for several years. Once they choose a site, the female is focused on building the nest, bringing in grasses, bark, and feathers to make it perfect.

photography by JH Williams / iStock / Getty Images Plus

LAZULI BUNTING
Passerina amoena
Cardinal family (Cardinalidae)

Quick ID: Male—sky blue; yellow under throat; white belly; white wing bars; black mask. Female—warm browns on head and back; lighter tan below; gray and brown on wings; light bill.

Length: 5–6" (13–15 cm)
Weight: 0.5–0.6 oz (13–18 g)
Wingspan: 8–9" (20–23 cm)

Showy and gorgeous, the blue lazuli bunting males are far more visible than the withdrawn and drabber females hanging out in the thicker cover. Lazuli buntings prefer south-facing slopes, and it's best to look for them in thickets along the forest edges, as well as near streams or brushy meadows. Caterpillars, beetles, spiders, and insects also thrive in these areas, and the buntings rely on serviceberries, as well as the seeds of herbaceous plants later in the season. They build their nests, typically only 3' (1 m) high, in the shrubs, where they raise three to four young—if the cowbirds don't monopolize the resources by laying an egg in the clutch.

AMERICAN ROBIN
Turdus migratorius
Thrush family (Turdidae)
Quick ID: Male—black head; gray wings and tail; bright orange belly; yellow bill. Female—more evenly gray on top; paler orange-rust below.
Length: 8–11" (20–28 cm)
Weight: 2.7–3 oz (77–85 g)
Wingspan: 12–16" (30–41 cm)

Robins are one of the most recognized species throughout North America, and are equally at home from the valleys to the higher elevations. It's not surprising to see robins pulling earthworms from the soil in the lawns of the lodges, along with plucking out other insects and sometimes snails, especially after a rain. Robins construct the classic bird nest design on a horizontal branch of a tree or shrub where they lay three to seven pale blue eggs. The hungry and demanding young keep both parents busy until they leave the nest at roughly two weeks old. Later in the season, their diet shifts to berries, and even though they are classic migratory species, some wintertime residents remain around West Glacier and Apgar.

USFWS

BULL TROUT

Salvelinus confluentus
Trout family (Salmonidae)

Quick ID: Yellowish or cream-colored distinct spots along silver-green back and sides; no black at all; no spots on the dorsal fin; slightly forked tail

Length: 6–32" (15–51 cm)

Weight: 0.5-25 lbs (0.27–11 kg)

This quintessentially native—and threatened—species of trout thrives in the cold streams, rivers, and lakes of Glacier and Waterton Lakes, but not without a little help. In order to meet the challenges, such as their potential hybridization with the non-native brook trout, resulting in sterile offspring, and being outcompeted by the voracious lake trout, managers are maintaining the bull trout's place in the ecosystem through relocation and lake trout suppression efforts. Bull trout spawn in their natal tributaries in the autumn once they reach four to six years old. The fry remain in the stream for one to two years, feeding upon mayflies, stoneflies, and other aquatic insects. By the time they're adults, they consume whitefish, sculpins, and other small fish.

WESTSLOPE CUTTHROAT TROUT
Oncorhynchus clarkii lewisi
Trout family (Salmonidae)
Quick ID: Red or orange slash at lower jaw; irregular black spots on back and sides; smaller, dark, and more-abundant spots near tail; black spots on dorsal fin
Length: 6–15" (15–38 cm)
Weight: 0.5–1.5 lbs (0.27–0.68 kg)

The westslope cutthroat is one of the two subspecies of native cutthroat trout in Montana, the other being the Yellowstone cutthroat trout (*Oncorhynchus clarkii bouvieri*), which were introduced to the ecosystem. As a species, there is concern due to food competition with non-native species, as well as potential hybridization with non-native rainbow trout, which results in the creation of a "cutbow" in many lakes and streams. The cutbow may feature traits of both species, with the coloration of the rainbow and the cutthroat's orange slash at the jawline, or it may be indistinguishable from other westslope cutthroats. This species spawns in June when the water levels begin receding, so there is some overlap with the rainbow trout spawning time. They feed upon aquatic insects and zooplankton throughout their life cycle.

RAINBOW TROUT
Oncorhynchus mykiss
Trout family (Salmonidae)
Quick ID: Blue-green overall color; pink along sides; light yellow underbelly; black spots on top of body, tail, and dorsal fin
Length: 6–18" (15–45 cm)
Weight: 0.5–2 lbs (0.27–0.9 kg)

Except for the redband rainbow, a native subspecies in the far north-western part of Montana, most rainbow trout were introduced for sport fishing in the late 1800s, long before genetic consistency was an issue. Rainbows prefer the same clean, cold lakes and streams as the westslope cutthroat trout, and have hybridized with a number of the populations. Rainbows are popular with anglers because they are quick to snag a fly or spinner. During spawning in the late spring to early summer, the female creates a depression in the gravel, called a redd, where she deposits the eggs that are then fertilized by a nearby male. The fry are prey for larger fish, kingfishers, otters, and mink, while grown trout are susceptible to predation from ospreys, eagles, and bigger fish.

slowmotiongli/ iStock / Getty Images Plus

LAKE TROUT
Salvelinus namaycush
Trout family (Salmonidae)
Quick ID: Green to dark coloration; light spots; tall dorsal fin; deeply forked tail
Length: 12–30" (30–76 cm)
Weight: 1–10 lbs (2.2–4.5 kg)

Lake trout are an example of how a native species in one area exists within a balance, while its presence in a new area means an upheaval of the ecosystem. Native lake trout of the Hudson Bay drainage, east of the Continental Divide, in areas such as Waterton Lakes, St. Mary Lake, as well as Glenn and Cosley Lakes, presents no issues with other native species. This is not the case on the west side. Introduced into Flathead Lake in 1905, lake trout eventually found their way to other lakes within Glacier, outeating and actually consuming native species such as bull trout. They feed upon zooplankton and aquatic insects when young, and eventually grow to prey on fish up to 15" (38 cm) in size. With the oldest recorded lake trout estimated at sixty-five years old, they can eat a lot of other fish in their lifetimes.

BROOK TROUT
Salvelinus fontinalis
Trout family (Salmonidae)

Quick ID: Light to olive green; red spots with bluish halos on sides; yellow spots on the sides leading to squiggly yellow markings on the back, black markings on the dorsal fin
Length: 6–12" (15–30 cm)
Weight: 0.5–1.5 lbs (227–680 g)

Introduced over a century ago as a sport fish, brook trout quickly established themselves throughout the region. Popular because of their beauty and spunk, anglers find them in lakes and streams in Waterton Lakes, Lake Sherburne, and Two Medicine, Pray, and Upper Two Medicine Lakes. Brook trout spawn in the autumn, with the eggs hatching in the early spring. They are efficient feeders, consuming aquatic insects, and at times, larger fish will eat the smaller ones. They are problematic within the Glacier and Waterton Lakes ecosystem because they can hybridize with bull trout, further degrading this threatened native species. Brook trout also outcompete the native westslope cutthroat trout for food and space, plus they feed upon cutthroat fry.

KOKANEE SALMON
Oncorhynchus nerka
Trout family (Salmonidae)
Quick ID: Silver most of its life; few black spots on back; moderately forked tail; turns bright red during spawning; males develop hooked jaw
Length: 8–15" (20–38 cm)
Weight: 1–2 lbs (454–907 g)

Much smaller than their ocean-dwelling relative, kokanee are the land-locked version of sockeye salmon. Introduced into Flathead Lake in 1914, they ultimately found their way to additional waters, including Lake McDonald. Prior to the 1980s, when the kokanee salmon spawned, hundreds of bald eagles and plenty of human observers came to the show. After the population crashed—because the mysis shrimp introduced as a food source ultimately outcompeted the salmon fry for zooplankton—the annual spectacle ceased. Remnant populations of kokanee remain on the west side of Glacier. Kokanee spawn in the late fall in the nearby tributaries and subsequently die. During this time, the males turn a bright red and develop a pronounced lower jaw, while the females take on a less-pronounced reddish hue.

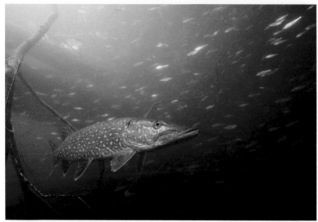

Yannick Tylle / iStock / Getty Images Plus

NORTHERN PIKE
Esox lucius
Pike family (Esocidae)
Quick ID: Olive green; light belly; light spots along back and sides; flattened, pointed snout; mouthful of sharp teeth
Length: 10–40" (25–102 cm)
Weight: 1.5–20 lbs (0.7–9 kg)

Pike receive a bad rap as being a voracious predator targeting vulnerable species, but they are perfectly at home in Lake Sherburne in Many Glacier, as well as in Waterton Lake. They cruise slowly and stealthily or sit completely still until a potential meal is detected within striking range. With their streamlined bodies, they streak exceptionally fast, swimming up to 8 mph (13 km/h) and grabbing their prey with their sharp teeth. Pike aren't picky eaters either, consuming frogs, birds, or other fish up to more than half their length. Shortly after the ice leaves the lakes, they spawn in vegetation in the shallow water along the shore, which is a good place for the fry and young fish to avoid being food for lake trout or other predatory fish in the deeper waters.

MOUNTAIN WHITEFISH
Prosopium williamsoni
Trout family (Salmonidae)
Quick ID: Silvery with large scales; light brown on back; slight overhanging snout; rounded mouth; no teeth; deeply forked tail
Length: 10–16" (25–41 cm)
Weight: 1–5 lbs (0.5–2.25 kg)

The Montana and Alberta native mountain whitefish are smaller than the introduced lake whitefish (*Coregonus clupeaformis*) that also live in the rivers and lakes of the region. While they might resemble a sucker with their overhanging snout, whitefish have a small fin in front of their tail. They are an important prey species for bull trout, and although they outnumber all species of trout in the same waters, their feeding habits are distinctly different. Mountain whitefish hang toward the bottom of the lake or river, eating aquatic insects, while trout hunt closer to the top. Both the lake and mountain whitefish ranges overlap to some degree in the fall and early winter, when large groups of the lake whitefish head to the rivers and streams to spawn.

Glacier NPS

ROCKY MOUNTAIN SCULPIN
Cottus bondi
Sculpin family (Cottidae)
Quick ID: Brown to dark brown on top and sides; light-colored belly; 2 spined dorsal fins; spiny side fins; bulging eyes
Length: 4–5" (10–13 cm)
Weight: 3–8 oz (85–227 g)

Rocky Mountain sculpins are so ugly they're almost cute. With heads too large for their bodies, frog-like eyes, and impressively spiked fins sticking out on their sides, tops, and bottoms, they're not sleek and sexy. Being bottom dwellers, they prefer fast-moving streams loaded with cobbles and rocks, giving them places to hide, along with prime areas to locate aquatic insect larvae, crustaceans, and fish eggs at night. Although they are more active after dark, they're sometimes observed foraging in shallow parts of the stream or river during the day. The smaller, only 1–2" (2–5 cm), and elusive deepwater sculpin (*Myoxocephalus thompsonii*) is documented in Upper Waterton Lake and the Hudson Bay drainage, but lives hundreds of feet/meters deep in the icy cold waters and is rarely seen.

ORCHARD GRASS
Dactylis glomerata
Grass family (Poaceae)
Quick ID: Flat, basal leaves 0.6–0.3" (4–8 mm) wide that taper toward the top; dense seed heads 1.6–8" (4–20 cm) long; green early in the season
Height: 31–40" (80–100 cm)
Bloom season: June–August

Orchard grass has been around so long it seems as if it's always been here. Originating in Europe, Asia, and North Africa, settlers brought it to North America in the mid-1700s as a livestock forage crop. Now it's found in pastures and ditches, as well as in the grasslands and roadsides of Glacier and Waterton Lakes. Many of the lower-elevation meadows, such as in St. Mary along Two Dog Flats, are interspersed with this valuable forage that elk and deer use throughout the season. Unlike other grasses that reach out with rhizomes, orchard grass spreads by the seeds that are dispersed when carried on clothing or animal fur, as well as to some extent by the wind.

COMMON TIMOTHY
Phleum pratense
Grasses family (Poaecea)
Quick ID: Dense, spikelike seed heads form on tall single stalks; thin leaves 4–12" (10–30 cm) long
Height: 20–40" (50–100 cm)
Bloom season: June–July

Non-native plants are part of the landscape, and common timothy was originally seeded as a forage crop for livestock long before anyone realized the problem of outside species. Elk and deer eat it as much as cows and horses, plus birds use the seed, but this vigorous bunchgrass still edges out native species. Although common timothy was brought in from other areas, alpine timothy (*Phleum alpinum*), found in moist areas in the subalpine to alpine regions, is a long-lived native also eaten by elk and deer. Standing only 2–6" (5–15 cm) tall, alpine timothy has a similar appearance to common timothy, with the same dense seed heads, although they are generally shorter and wider, and their leaves reach to the top of the stem.

IDAHO FESCUE
Festuca idahoensis
Grass family (Poaceae)
Quick ID: Wispy green to bluish-green leaves, 12–24" (30–61 cm) long; grows in clumps; slender seed heads
Height: 10–31" (25–80 cm)
Bloom season: June–August

Idaho fescue is an abundant and important cool-season bunchgrass for a wide range of wildlife. Elk utilize it as forage in the winter, and mule deer turn to this source in the spring. It retains its nutritional value in the winter, even though it flops over and looks dead. Birds and small rodents feed upon the seeds. Mice eat the foliage, as well as use the dense plants as cover, since the clumps of this grass are easily 12" (30 cm) across and usually grow in groups among the other vegetation. Because it has a deep root system, Idaho fescue grows well in arid conditions and poor soils. Another native species, shortleaf fescue (*Festuca brachyphylla*), is about half the size of the Idaho fescue and grows in higher, rockier terrain.

COMMON CATTAIL
Typha latifolia
Cattail family (Typhaceae)
Quick ID: Brown, cigar-shaped spike on top of sturdy stem with long, lance-shaped leaves
Height: 4–7' (1–2 m)
Bloom season: June–August

The cattail is recognized as the classic wetland plant found throughout North America, but it's not known for its blooms. Cattail flowers are definitely different. The female part is the cigar-shaped brown formation on top of the stem. The male flowering sections are yellow and are attached to spike above the female part. When the formation "poofs," the lightweight seed capsules attached to the little tufts of fluff travel on the wind, settle on the water, and float to a new location. Cattails are edible for humans and wildlife, and have long been used as a source for food and medicine. Waterfowl and muskrats eat the nutritious shoots and starchy roots. Marsh wrens and yellow-headed and red-winged blackbirds nest and live among the reeds, and many other birds use the fluff from the flowers to build their nests.

HORSETAIL
Equisetum arvense
Horsetail family (Equisetum)
Quick ID: Hollow, segmented stems; gritty texture; whorled foliage looks like a vertical brush on the top of the stem
Height: 3–12" (8–30 cm)
Bloom season: March–June

A close inspection of horsetails is a peek into the prehistoric landscape with a primitive life cycle that has lasted far longer than most species. As the snow recedes from near the roads and open areas, brown, spore-bearing stalks push through the cold ground, followed shortly by the green vegetative stalks resembling a bristly tail. These ancient plants reproduce by spores as well as spreading rhizomes, which can reach several feet into the ground, one of the many reasons this plant has survived for millennia. They are a valuable early-season and protein-rich food source for black bears and grizzlies that graze upon the young shoots before they develop too much silica in the stems and lose a lot of their nutritional value. This abrasive element is how it earned another common name, scouring rush.

146

SATYR COMMA
Polygonia satyrus
Brush-footed Butterfly family (Nymphalidae)

Quick ID: Tawny to golden orange coloration; black dots on either side of the body; series of dark dots and markings; scalloped, brown-tinted wing edges

Wingspan: 2–2.5" (0.8–1 cm)

Flight season: April–July

Early in the season, open forests, particularly near streams or lakes, come alive with these colorful butterflies after they emerge from their winter dormancy to look for mates. Food can be scarce at this time of the year, so it's not uncommon to see clusters of satyr commas covering dung piles to acquire important nutrients such as nitrogen and sodium, particularly during the breeding season. Satyr commas prefer stinging nettle as a host plant, and the female lays eggs on the underside of the leaves, where the caterpillars wrap themselves and feed as they grow. Adults mature in the late summer and early fall, and feed upon nectar and tree sap before crawling into a protected space to spend the winter.

PAINTED LADY
Vanessa cardui
Brush-footed Butterfly family (Nymphalidae)
Quick ID: Upper surface of wing is orange, brown, black, and white; black with white markings on tips of forewings; 5 brown spots on edge of hind wing; slightly fuzzy brown to orangish body
Wingspan: 2–3" (5–9 cm)
Flight season: May–October

A globally widespread butterfly, the painted lady is a beautiful sight among the wildflowers of Glacier, and in some years their migration reaches beyond southern Alberta when rainy conditions in the Southern states and Mexico, where they originate, cause them to fly farther north. Found in open meadows and sunny areas ranging from the valleys to alpine elevations, they're visible throughout the summer, feeding upon practically any nectar-producing flower. The females lay pale green eggs that grow into intimidating-looking dark purple to black caterpillars sporting yellow or green stripes. The spines along their back and sides make them less palatable to predators. The caterpillars pupate by weaving themselves within a silky cocoon upon the host plant, such as a thistle, emerging as an adult ten days later.

MOURNING CLOAK
Nymphalis antiopa
Brush-footed Butterfly family (Nymphalidae)
Quick ID: Rich, brownish-maroon wings with blue dots along the outer margin; wings are outlined on the outside edge in cream
Wingspan: 3–3.5" (7.6–9 cm)
Flight season: April–September

The official butterfly of the State of Montana is one of the first species to emerge, flying on warm days before the snow is melted. They frequently sun themselves on a rock or against the bark of a tree, blending in extremely well on the latter. Males stake out specific territories and approach females who venture within their range. The female lays a cluster of several dozen pale yellow eggs on host plants such as willows and cottonwoods, and after the larvae emerge, they feed together in groups. The dark-colored, 2"-long (5-cm-long) caterpillars with tiny white dots look imposing with their courses of prickly spikes. After they pupate, the adults feed several weeks, often visible on sunny days even into September, before they tuck themselves behind bark or another protected space to spend the winter.

GILLETT'S CHECKERSPOT
Euphydryas gillettii
Brush-footed Butterfly family (Nymphalidae)
Quick ID: Orange overall; black-and-white checkerboard markings; black body; rounded wings; orange-red band near the outside of the wings
Wingspan: 1.5–2" (4–5 cm)
Flight season: June–August

In the high mountain meadows, the Gillett's checkerspot takes advantage of the brief yet glorious profusion of wildflowers to complete its life cycle. A similar species, the Edith's checkerspot (*Euphydryas editha*), is more prevalent in the parks, and the easiest way to tell them apart is the red-orange band near the top edge of the wings of the Gillett's checkerspot. There are a few pockets of Gillett's checkerspot butterflies in the region, and colonies tend to stay close to their original range, as it may take a couple of seasons for the butterflies to mature. Females lay eggs on the underside of the leaves of host plants, such as twinberry honeysuckle or snowberries, and the caterpillars create silk nests to feed before hibernating after an initial molting. They develop into an adult after the fifth molting the following season.

Glacier NPS

ROCKY MOUNTAIN CLEARWING MOTH
Hemaris thetis
Sphynx and Hawk Moth family (Sphingidae)
Quick ID: Fuzzy brown body; light patch toward end of the body; clear, long forewings and short hind wings outlined with dark band; distinct antennae
Wingspan: 0.6–0.7" (15–17 mm)
Flight season: June–August

Looking like a busy bumblebee visiting flowers throughout the day, the Rocky Mountain clearwing moth is a clever mimic with its 1–1.75" (3–4.5 cm) transparent wings giving away its identity. These gentle and fuzzy-looking moths are found in mixed forests from the lower elevations to subalpine regions. They act like a bumblebee when approaching a flower, but instead of climbing within the flower, they hover just outside of the blossoms of lupine, thistles, and kinnikinnick to collect the nectar. The bright green, roughly 1.25"-long (3-cm-long) caterpillars have a horn and spots along the side and are more-specific feeders, focusing on snowberries and honeysuckle foliage. They eventually form a cocoon tucked among the leaf litter and forest debris to pupate into an adult.

LADYBIRD BEETLES
Coccinella spp.
Ladybird Beetle family (Coccinellidae)
Quick ID: Oval; orangish to dark red in color; 3 lines of black bands along back; pale head with black band
Size: 0.16–0.3" (4–7mm)
Flight season: April–October

Most people picture ladybird beetles, also called ladybugs, as the classic oval-shaped, red or bright orange body with black spots, and while many species share these classic characteristics, some step out of the stereotypical image. The 3-banded ladybug, *Coccinella trifasciata*, has the same shape and general coloration, although sometimes are a paler orange than expected. Instead of spots, there are three rows of black bands, sometimes with a gap in the center, along its shiny back. The small, alligator-looking larvae feed upon aphids and other small insects. Within the parks, watch for the 9-spotted ladybug, *Coccinella novemnotata*, which was once one of the most prevalent ladybug species throughout North America, yet has practically disappeared from many Eastern states and provinces. National parks may be this classic beetle's final stronghold.

Jim Hudgins, USFWS

COMMON GREEN DARNER

Anax junius

Darners family (Aeshnidae)

Quick ID: Male—green body with blue on the sides of their abdomen; purple stripe on its back; transparent wings. Female—more of a grayish-green color overall, with gray to purple abdomens; spot on forehead; transparent wings.

Size: 2.5–3" (7–8 cm)

Flight season: June–October

It's difficult to miss these chunky dragonflies in wetlands or meadows. In Montana and Alberta, there are resident green darners, as well as those that migrate from the southern United States and arrive before residents emerge. These migratory dragonflies breed in June to give the naiads enough time to develop before leaving prior to the winter. The residents mate in June or July, with the males and females depositing the eggs in tandem, a unique feature for dragonflies, on the vegetation below the water. Once the naiads complete their nymphal stage, which might take up to a year for the residents, they crawl out of the water to shed their skin and emerge as an adult.

WATER STRIDER
Gerris spp.
Water Strider family (Gerridae)
Quick ID: Black body; 4 long legs; 2 shorter legs near the head
Size: 0.4–0.6" (11–16 mm)
Season: April–October

Children, and those who are young at heart, are consistently fascinated by water striders as they watch them gliding effortlessly over the surface of slow-moving water. The combination of water-surface tension and thousands of microscopic, water-resistant hairs allows them to move as if they're flying on top of the water, although they can't walk on firm ground. Water striders are predators of small insects that live in or land on the water, including their own nymphs if they happen to venture too close to the adult. They also consume dead insects, making them an important part of this small ecosystem. Looking at a water strider, it's obvious that the long legs are built for movement, but the shorter front legs grab their prey. They use a specialized mouthpart called a proboscis to pierce the insect and consume its juices.

BUMBLEBEE
Bombus spp.
Bee family (Apidae)
Quick ID: Robust, black and yellow fuzzy body; 4 wings
Size: 0.4–1" (11–25 mm)
Flight season: April–October

There are dozens of bumblebees in the region, and while certain species might be difficult to pinpoint, bumblebees are easy to identify by their fuzzy, striped appearance. Commonly seen in meadows and open forests, they are not particularly picky, utilizing penstemons, asters, thistle blossoms, and spirea blooms throughout the season. Shortly after the snow melts, solitary queens emerge from their hibernacula where they've spent the winter, providing a valuable pollination service to early-blooming plants. At this time, each queen searches for a suitable nest, which is often in abandoned rodent tunnels or debris piles. When she lays the eggs, she keeps them warm with her abdomen, only venturing out briefly to feed. It takes approximately four weeks until the young emerge as workers. Bumblebees are extremely gentle while on flowers, and will only sting if accidentally pinched or the nest is disturbed.

STONEFLY
Megarcys spp.
Common Stonefly family (Perlodidae)
Quick ID: 2 long antennae; 6 legs; brown to dark coloration; 2 tail-like structures on rear
Size: 0.2–2" (5–50 mm)
Season: May–September

Stoneflies make up a large family, with roughly one hundred species within Glacier and Waterton Lakes. While it might be difficult to distinguish individual species, they are part of the larger order of Plecoptera and have many common characteristics. Most are found in cold, swift stream habitats and lakes. They are predators with strong mandibles and a dual forked tail-like structure called cerci, yet are equally subject to predation by fish and birds. There is cause for concern about the future of a couple of species due to changing habitat within the region. The western glacier stonefly (*Zapada glacier*) and the meltwater stonefly (*Lednia tumana*) rely on alpine, glacier-fed streams, and are moving to higher locations as the temperatures warm. Both species occupy the first 0.5 mile (0.8 km) of the water source and need temperatures below 43 degrees F (6.3 C) to survive.

BLACK CARPENTER ANT
Camponotus pennsylvanicus
Ant family (Formicidae)
Quick ID: Shiny black; rounded thorax; winged or wingless; 6 legs, 2 antennae
Size: 0.25–0.75" (6–19 mm)
Season: March–November

Carpenter ants receive a bad rap when they chew into buildings or wooden structures, but as part of the natural cycle they are perfect at breaking down logs and old trees. They don't eat wood, but rather tunnel through it to create their colonies. Their primary food sources are other insects, including dead ones. They also utilize the "honeydew" (liquid waste) created by aphids. In the spring, large, winged unmated females are most visible, with the nuptial flight of thousands of ants taking to the air to mate, creating a dramatic show. This is also a feast for birds, fish, and other animals. When an ant female successfully mates, she builds a nest in soft wood to start a new colony, raising daughters that don't grow wings due to a particular chemical she secretes, although eventually, new unmated females develop to continue the cycle.

ROCKY MOUNTAIN WOOD TICK
Dermacentor andersoni
Hard Ticks family (Ixodidae)
Quick ID: Brown to reddish-brown; dark markings on back; 8 legs; pear-shaped
Size: 0.1–0.2" (2–6 mm)
Season: March–August

No one wants to find a tick, but it's important to check for them after every outing in Glacier or Waterton Lakes starting as early as March and well into summer. Found in mid- to higher elevations, it's easy to pick them up after resting on the ground or traveling through thick vegetation. Rocky Mountain wood ticks are known vectors for Rocky Mountain spotted fever and tularemia, and people should seek medical attention if they develop symptoms after being bitten by one. Breeding typically occurs in May and June, and while these are not fast-growing arachnids, taking one to three years to go through all of their stages of life, it all starts with the bred female feeding until satiated before falling off her host. Afterward, she'll lay anywhere from 2,500 to more than 7,000 eggs on the ground over several weeks before dying.

WOLF SPIDER
Pardosa spp.
Wolf Spider family (Lycosidae)
Quick ID: Mottled, dark brown; thin legs; 8 eyes
Size: 0.2–0.5" (6–12 mm)
Season: April–September

Wolf spiders make a big impression because they act as if they're not afraid of anyone or anything. Although they are bold, they are typically not aggressive unless provoked, and their bite is not deadly. Notice the three rows of their eight total eyes, as well as the pedipalps, which look like tiny legs in the front, which they use to grab prey. The pedipalps are more prominent in the males. Even though black widows are notorious for killing their mates, ending up as food is a possibility for male wolf spiders when they approach a female, particularly if she is unfamiliar with his physical appearance. After breeding, the female spins a sac and carries it until the spiderlings hatch. Wolf spiders don't spin webs, instead burrowing into the ground or hiding beneath rocks to ambush their prey, including ants and any small invertebrate.

COMMON HARVESTMAN
Phalangium opilio
Harvestman family (Phalangiidae)
Quick ID: Brown; oval-shaped body; 8 long legs
Size: 1.5–2" (4–5 cm)
Season: April–November

Commonly called daddy long legs, the harvestman is an arachnid but not a spider. They're more closely related to mites, with all eight of their legs attaching to their single, oval-shaped body. They also have two eyes instead of eight. Some spiders, like the cellar spiders of the Pholcidae family, are also called daddy long legs. They have two body segments, produce venom, and can spin webs. The myth that daddy long legs, including cellar spiders, are the most venomous spiders to people is false. The common harvestman, a non-native species to this area, is found in grasslands and forests, scavenging fungi, dead insects, and decaying matter. They will lose a leg as a means of self-protection, although if the second pair is damaged, the harvestman dies. To further discourage predators, a gland behind their first set of legs produces a vinegary-smelling substance.

VitalisG/ iStock /Getty Images Plus

GOLDENROD CRAB SPIDER
Misumena vatia
Crab Spider family (Thomisidae)
Quick ID: Crab-like appearance; short, rounded body; large, open forelegs; can be white, yellow, or green
Size: 0.1–0.4" (39 mm)
Season: May–September

Take a close look before sniffing the flowers in the parks, since crab spiders are camouflage masters, blending into blossoms while waiting for their next meal. Crab spiders are ambush predators, changing their coloration to blend in with the flowers, which might take several weeks. A white spider on bear grass will turn a bright yellow to blend in with the goldenrod later in the season. When an insect lands on the blossom, the crab spider dashes out and grabs it with its strong front legs, immobilizing it with its venom before sucking out the insect's juices. Bees, flies, and butterflies are typical meals. When it's time for the female to lay eggs, she creates a protective pocket by folding over a bit of a leaf and spinning it closed. The spiderlings look like tiny versions of the adults.

BEAR GRASS
Xerophyllum tenax
Bunchflower family (Melanthiaceae)
Quick ID: Large globe of tiny, star-shaped white flowers atop the tall stalk; large mound of evergreen, grasslike leaves
Height: 3–5' (0.90–1.5 m)
Bloom season: May–July

Bear grass takes center stage with a riot of hundreds of tiny white blossoms forming an elongated globe on top of stately, sturdy stalks. Those who can't resist sniffing the mildly sweet-smelling bloom often unwittingly walk away with a pollen mustache. Individual plants bloom every three to seven years in the lower elevations and subalpine slopes beginning as early as May, continuing well into July in the higher elevations. The clumps of rough, grasslike leaves remain green throughout the year. Bear grass is a yearlong food source for rodents, as well as sheep and goats, and bears are known to use its pithy stalks for bedding in their dens. Being the unofficial wildflower of both parks, look for enormous sweeps of bear grass throughout Glacier, as well as along Waterton Lakes' Akamina Parkway.

PEARLY EVERLASTING
Anaphalis margaritacea
Aster family (Asteraceae)
Quick ID: Clusters of white flower heads with yellow centers when fully open; narrow gray-green, fuzzy leaves
Height: 10–24" (25–61 cm)
Bloom season: June–September

Despite the seemingly delicate, jewellike reference in its name, pearly everlastings are tough. They tolerate disturbed, gravelly soil in arid environments as well as the more-temperate conditions of open forests, from valleys to subalpine regions. Growing in small clumps, early in the season the small flower heads are closed tightly in pure white, shiny clusters; later, when they open, they develop a more-flattened appearance. Their beautiful white, petallike bracts (which are modified leaves) surround the yellow flower center. Pearly everlasting has distinct male and female flowers on separate plants, so they rely on cross-pollination from bees, butterflies, moths, and other insects. Even after the flowers die, these pretty white blooms stand tall until winter.

ROUNDLEAF ALUMROOT
Heuchera cylindrica
Saxifrage family (Saxifragaceae)
Quick ID: Oval to heart-shaped basal leaves; cream-colored, bell-shaped flowers with 5 lobes form spikes on the top of the leafless stem
Height: 6–32" (15–81 cm)
Bloom season: May–July

Roundleaf alumroot blooms at the same time as the Alberta penstemons, yellow columbines, and Indian paintbrush. This drought-tolerant plant grows from the valleys to the tree-line regions in dry forests, although it also thrives near seeps or streams. It continues to bloom in the higher elevations as the season progresses. Bees love the somewhat sticky, cup-shaped flowers, and are important for the pollination of the plant. Each one is anchored by sturdy rhizomes forming a dense crown, but they rely on seed dispersal to spread. The deep green leaves at the base of the plant have five to seven slightly hairy, leathery lobes with a similar appearance as the domesticated coral bells, another member of the *Heuchera* genus, and the roundleaf alumroot has the same vigorous and beautiful nature.

THREELEAF FOAMFLOWER
Tiarella trifoliata
Saxifrage family (Saxifragaceae)
Quick ID: Open cluster of star-shaped, white flowers spread out at the top part of the stem; 3-lobed leaves at the base of the plant
Height: 6–20" (15–48 cm)
Bloom season: May–July

Found in the shade of coniferous forests to sunnier subalpine meadows, often where thimbleberries and queen's cup beadlilies thrive, foamflowers illuminate the understory with their tiny, loosely branched flowers on slender stems that reach up to a foot (30 cm) above the palmated leaves clustered at the base. On their own, foamflowers are beautiful, but they're particularly striking growing in groups among the wintergreen or where the water seeps from the rocks. Only 0.25" (6 mm) wide, having a hand lens or being able to zoom in with a phone is the best way to appreciate the downward-facing, delicate five-petaled blooms that look like tiny stars. Plants spread slowly through rhizomes, as well as the seeds that are dispersed by birds and rodents.

MOUNTAIN DEATH CAMAS
Anticlea elegans
Bunchflower family (Melanthiaceae)
Quick ID: White to cream-colored flower consisting of 6 oval petallike tepals; slender leaves at the base of the plant
Height: 6–25" (15–63 cm)
Bloom season: July–August

Mountain death camas grows from grasslands, including the bison paddock in Waterton Lakes, to open forests and subalpine areas. This delicate-looking plant boasts cream-colored, 0.75"-wide (19-mm-wide) flowers with a green heart-shaped gland at the center of each blossom. They bloom in small clusters along the leafless stem above a clump of slender, grasslike foliage. Consuming just two of the bulbs can be fatal to humans, and livestock sometimes inadvertently poison themselves by accidentally grazing upon this plant (or one of the several varieties in the region), as all parts of the plant are toxic. The bulbs are potentially confused with the nutritious blue camas (*Camassia quamash*), although the cream-colored flowers of the death camas are distinctly different from the starry blue or purple blooms of the blue camas.

QUEENCUP BEADLILY
Clintonia uniflora
Lily family (Liliaceae)
Quick ID: White, star-shaped flower with 6 petallike sepals; 2 to 3 large, shiny, deep green basal leaves
Height: 3–8" (8–20 cm)
Bloom season: May–July

This semi-succulent plant with two to three large leaves growing at the base of the single, flower-bearing stem brightens the coniferous wood-lands of the western cedar and western hemlock to the subalpine fir forests. The pure white, petallike sepals open into a star-shaped 1"-wide (2-cm-wide) flower. It is also called "bride's bonnet" because of its bright appearance. The flowers are particularly striking when they blanket the area with their deep green foliage and white blossoms, often growing alongside mariposa lilies and threeleaf foamflowers in the early summer. Queencup beadlilies are not edible for humans, but ruffed grouse, varied thrush, and sometimes elk and deer consume the smooth, blue berries, measuring 0.25–0.4" wide (6–10 mm wide) and containing five to seven seeds per berry.

POINTEDTIP MARIPOSA LILY
Calochortus apiculatus
Lily family (Liliaceae)

Quick ID: Cup-shaped flower with 3 creamy white petals; yellow at the center with black spot on the base of each petal; single, slender leaf at base

Height: 6–12" (15–30 cm)

Bloom season: June–July

Meaning "butterfly" in Spanish, *mariposa* is a good way to remember this beautiful flower, which is a favorite of butterflies and other insects. A long, flat leaf is found at the base of the plant, and the single stem holds this dainty three-petaled blossom upright for everyone to enjoy. Upon closer observation, notice the tiny hairs on the petals close to the center. The black spot, a gland at the base of each petal, is a distinctive characteristic of this early summer flower. It's found in open conifer and mixed forests, as well as sunny meadows from the valleys to subalpine areas. It's sometimes confused with trillium because of the three petals, but trilliums bloom a month earlier and the leaves are wider.

SITKA VALERIAN
Valeriana sitchensis
Valerian family (Valerianaceae)
Quick ID: Clusters of small, white flowers; paired leaves with 3 to 9 elongated lobes
Height: 10–29" (25–74 cm)
Bloom season: June–August

Valerian is difficult to miss at the height of the wildflower season, as it fills entire meadows with its dainty white blooms that are sometimes tinged with pink, along with the two to five pairs of deeply lobed leaves with scalloped edges along the stem. It thrives in forests, avalanche chutes, and the alpine regions that stay consistently damp, even in the heat of the summer, such as in the area near Twin Lakes in Waterton Lakes. The Sitka valerian's blossoms do not have the strong fragrance of the domestic valerian, although the roots boast the same sleep-inducing—and foul-smelling—qualities used as a mild sedative for generations. Like many of the plants with umbrella-like clusters of flowers, butterflies and other native insects are regularly found on the blossoms.

YARROW
Achillea millefolium
Aster family (Asteraceae)
Quick ID: Tiny white flowers form flat clusters; narrow, lacy, fernlike flowers; strong medicinal smell
Height: 7–24" (18–61 cm)
Bloom season: May–September

Yarrow is a well-adapted herb found along roadsides or other disturbed areas, along with prairies and open forests, and is particularly abundant in lower-elevation meadows. It blooms from the late spring and continues until frost. Notice the tiny—less than 0.25" (6 mm)—white flowers with yellow centers that are tightly grouped to form the flat cluster. Yarrow attracts a wide variety of bees, beetles, and butterflies, providing a terrific opportunity to observe these fascinating creatures. Larger animals, such as bighorn sheep and deer, browse upon it even though it has a sharp fragrance. In historical lore, yarrow is a potent medicinal plant, as the genus *Achillea* refers to Achilles, the Greek hero who derived his protection from the plant. Historically, it's been used as a poultice to treat wounds, stop bleeding, and fight infections.

CANADIAN BUNCHBERRY
Cornus canadensis
Dogwood family (Cornaceae)
Quick ID: 4 petallike white bracts; evergreen whorls of oval, pointed leaves; bright red berry cluster in the fall
Height: 2–8" (5–20 cm)
Bloom season: May–July

Canadian bunchberry forms a beautiful mat of evergreen leaves and bright flowers, and is found in dappled forests, in avalanche chutes, and along open areas on the edges of forests. What looks like perfect, four-petaled white flowers are actually specialized leaves that hold the extraordinarily tiny greenish-white quartet of petals that come together when closed. Zoom in with a phone for a closer look. It's during its pollination by bumblebees or other native, solitary bees that the magic happens. There is a hairlike trigger at the top of the petals, and when a bee touches it, the flower bursts open, dusting pollen onto the bee as the bee simultaneously drops any pollen it collected from other bunchberry plants. The results are the bright red berries utilized by ruffed grouse, snowshoe hares, and black bears.

PACIFIC TRILLIUM
Trillium ovatum
Bunchflower family (Melanthiaceae)
Quick ID: 3 white petals on top of an individual stem, with the petals turning pink after a few days; 3 egg-shaped leaves at the base of the plant
Height: 6–14" (15–36 cm)
Bloom season: April–June

Appearing early in the spring in moist, wooded areas, the three leaves and three petals are a welcome sight. Trillium plants are at least eighteen years old before they first bloom, and the oldest known plant in the Pacific Northwest was seventy-two years old. Although they are a rhizomatous perennial, they primarily reproduce through seed production, and must be cross-pollinated by bees and beetles visiting the flowers on different plants. Insects are critical in planting the seeds, with an ingenious means of dispersal. At the end of each seed there is a yellow, fatty, protein-rich nodule called an elaiosome. This nutritious food source entices ants to carry the seed to their nest, where they consume the nodule yet leave the seed, starting a new plant.

STARRY FALSE SOLOMON'S-SEAL
Maianthemum stellatum
Asparagus family (Asparagaceae)
Quick ID: White, tiny star-shaped blooms; pointed leaves on an arching stem; immature green berry with stripes that ripens to bright red
Height: 4–16" (10–41 cm)
Bloom season: May–June

Found in open forests on both sides of the divide, starry false Solomon's-seal is appreciated for its beautiful foliage, along with the star-shaped flowers that aren't even true flowers, as the white pseudo-petals are actually tepals. They form an eye-catching design that is appreciated up close, particularly since they are less than 0.3" (7 mm) wide. The elliptically shaped leaves have parallel veining and taper down to a pointed end. Various insects use the flowers for nectar, songbirds feed on the berries, and deer browse the foliage. Starry false Solomon's-seal looks similar to the feathery false Solomon's-seal (*Maianthemum racemosum*), although the latter has larger leaves and a more plumelike flower cluster.

WHITE BOG ORCHID
Platanthera dilatata
Orchid family (Orchidaceae)

Quick ID: Dozens of white blooms with 2 sepals on either side and a distinct hood at the top of the flower; long, liplike petal at base of bloom; succulent-looking, lance-shaped leaves point upward

Height: 12–24" (30–61 cm)

Bloom season: June–September

Many people are surprised to learn there are orchids in Glacier and Waterton Lakes, but the white bog orchid is only one of over twenty native species in the region. A striking plant with a sturdy stalk, the 2–6"- long (5–15-cm-long) leaves reach roughly halfway up the stem just below where the flowers begin. The flowers have a pleasant, somewhat spicy, fragrance, and offer a sweet nectar reward in their pouches for moths, bees, flies, and butterflies. Even though they are just 0.5" (1 cm) across, the flowers are strikingly exotic-looking, particularly close-up. They're found in sunny areas near streams and seeps along the trails, as well as in wetlands and fens.

MOUNTAIN LADY'S SLIPPER
Cypripedium montanum
Orchid family (Orchidaceae)
Quick ID: Bulbous, slipper-shaped white lower petal; trio of tress-like, brownish-purple upper petals; 2–6"-long (5–15-cm-long) leaves that are pointed
Height: 8–24" (20–61 cm)
Bloom season: May–July

The mountain lady's slipper is a delightful orchid to find, as you can easily imagine a tiny foot fitting into the nearly perfect white "slipper" that makes up the lower lip of the flower. Usually each plant produces one to two flowers, although there can be up to three, and the 0.75–1" (2–3 cm) pouch is tinged with purple veining inside of the petal. There are two brownish-purple twisted lateral petals radiating from the side and a similarly colored sepal at the top. As with other orchids, there is a connection between the fungal network within the soil and the orchids' survival, which is why they die when transplanted. The mountain lady's slippers thrive in drier conditions of open forests than many other orchids.

RED BANEBERRY
Actaea rubra
Buttercup family (Ranunculaceae)

Quick ID: Tiny white flowers with 5 to 10 petals on each; flower clusters are as tall as they are wide; multiple 3-toothed leaves; glossy red or white berries

Height: 11–31" (28–79 cm)

Bloom season: May–July

Red baneberry prefers the moist habitats near streams or among the forest understories, as well as aspen groves from valleys to subalpine areas. Blooming early in the summer, multiple tiny flowers form the flower cluster perched upon the sturdy stem, standing out against the large, wide-toothed leaves. As the season progresses, berries form in a fairly tight group. These 0.15–0.3" (4–7 mm) berries are shiny and inviting, but do not eat them. They are highly poisonous, especially to children. Although all parts of the baneberry are toxic to humans, elk eat the foliage after a frost because it remains green, and birds, including robins and grouse, consume the berries. They're also utilized by deer mice, squirrels, and chipmunks.

WHITE THISTLE
Cirsium hookerianum
Aster family (Asteraceae)
Quick ID: Spiny basal lance-looking leaves with weblike, silvery hairs; large flower heads with clusters of white florets grouped together at the top of the plant
Height: 8–36" (20–91 cm)
Bloom season: June–August

Not all thistles are bad characters. White thistle, which is also known as elk thistle, is a native found in open forests and meadows such as in the Two Medicine, St. Mary, and the Cut Bank regions, as well as along the Red Rock Parkway in Waterton Lakes. Pointed leaves loaded with prickly spikes are classic thistle characteristics, but unlike other species, the foliage is woolly. The drab, white flowers turn into the tufted seed heads, and while the first thought is to avoid it, it's important to understand its value. Local tribes on both sides of the mountains have long utilized it as a food source. White thistle is equally important to native pollinators, and headless stalks are usually the result of moose, elk, or deer grazing upon them.

WILD STRAWBERRY
Fragaria virginia
Rose family (Rosaceae)
Quick ID: 5 white petals with a yellow center form a cup-shaped flower; fuzzy stalk; 3-lobed, oval, slightly toothed leaves; red fruit
Height: 2–6" (5–15 cm)
Bloom season: May–July

Visitors are often surprised to see such a familiar plant springing up along the trail. Found in open forests, as well as in meadows, wild strawberries grow equally well in sun to partial shade and don't require the high moisture requirements of domestic strawberries. The bright white flowers are common along trails in the early summer, and depend upon bees and butterflies for pollination. The less than 0.5"-long (1-cm-long) fruit is dotted with tiny seeds, but the strawberries spread more effectively through their runners that reach out sideways from the plant, rooting where they touch the soil. The fruit begins ripening by mid-July in the lower elevations. Chipmunks, squirrels, grouse, and even bears graze upon wild strawberries during the summer, often before other berries are mature.

COW PARSNIP
Heracleum sphondylium ssp. *montanum*
Carrot family (Apiaceae)
Quick ID: White flowers form hand-size umbrellalike clusters; large, wide, 3-lobed leaves; hollow stems
Height: 2.5–7' (0.75–2 m)
Bloom season: May–August

Found in the open forests and on the edge of meadows, cow parsnip is impossible to miss. With massive leaves and white, flat flower clusters atop thick stems, it's as big as many shrubs. In the heat of the summer, the lush plants hold in the humidity, creating a veritable tunnel of foliage. It's wise to make extra noise when traveling through these dense areas of vegetation, as it's difficult to watch for bears. Deer, elk, and moose also browse on the tender vegetation. Coming in contact with the prickly stems and sap can cause dermatitis, yet the inside of the stem is edible. A word of caution: Poison hemlock (*Conium maculatum*) is similar in appearance and grows in much of the same habitat, so it's advisable not to touch it.

HEART-LEAVED ARNICA
Arnica cordifolia
Aster family (Asteraceae)
Quick ID: Bright yellow ray flowers with a yellow center disk; lance-shaped, often fuzzy, leaves
Height: 8–20" (20–50 cm)
Bloom season: June–August

With over a dozen arnica varieties found within the parks, one of the most common is the heart-leaved arnica, as well as its close relative, the broad-leaf or mountain arnica (*Arnica latifolia*). The latter has wider leaves in the middle of the plant, whereas the bottom leaves of the heart-leaved arnica are larger. Yet they are difficult to tell apart, particularly since they both have similar leaves with toothed margins. Another clue is that the broadleaf arnica's leaves attach directly to the stem, while the heart-leaved arnica has small stems (called petioles) connecting the leaves to the main stem. Both are found in open forests, especially after burns, to sunnier areas near streams or where water seeps from the rocks. Heart-leaved arnica rebounds well after wildfires, and recolonizes areas through their spreading rhizomes and seed dispersal.

ARROWLEAF BALSAMROOT
Balsamorhiza sagittata
Aster family (Asteraceae)
Quick ID: Large, bright yellow flowers on single stems; large, silvery-gray heart-shaped leaves
Height: 16–30" (41–76 cm)
Bloom season: May–June

In the spring, arrowleaf balsamroot takes center stage as it blooms in large, colorful displays on hillsides, or tucked into open ponderosa pine and aspen forests. Besides being a delight to view, they are an important food source, as the young foliage consists of 30 percent protein content utilized by bighorn sheep, elk, and deer, who favor the luscious, big blooms. Native pollinators are equally drawn to the showy flowers, and Columbian ground squirrels, along with other rodents and birds, utilize the sunflower-like seeds. The long taproots can be 8' (2 m) deep, and are one reason the plants thrive in the harsh, arid conditions. Photograph, don't pick, these gorgeous blooms on open slopes, near aspen groves, or in the open meadows around St. Mary, plus along the Red Rock Parkway and the Kootenai Brown Trail in Waterton Lakes.

SCOULER'S ST. JOHNSWORT
Hypericum scouleri
St. Johnswort family (Hypericaceae)
Quick ID: Yellow buds are tinged in pink; 5-petaled yellow flowers with numerous, tall stamens radiating from the center; small, oblong leaves
Height: 3–8" (7–20 cm)
Bloom season: June–September

The diminutive Scouler's St. Johnswort isn't a botanical bully like its relative, common St. Johnswort, which has a tendency to overtake meadows and disturbed areas. Found in seeps, wet meadows, and alongside streams, Scouler's St. Johnswort is easy to miss, although keep an eye open when walking in subalpine areas with ample sunshine and water. This native plant spreads by a rhizomatous root system, unlike the reseeding nature of common St. Johnswort. The flowers appear at the end of several smaller lateral branches, and there are usually varying degrees of maturing buds and flowers. Upon close inspection, notice the tiny black dots rimming the edges of the bright yellow flowers that grow in clusters on the short stems. The stamens reach well beyond the flowers, reminiscent of a tiny fireworks display.

BLANKETFLOWER
Gaillardia aristata
Aster family (Asteraceae)

Quick ID: Yellow flower heads with orange to reddish disk flowers in the center; coarse hairs on leaves and stems

Height: 12–24" (30–61 cm)

Bloom season: July–September

A highly versatile and hardy perennial, blanketflower is found from lower-elevation meadows to open forests in subalpine areas. The 3–6" (6–15 cm) fuzzy, gray-green leaves are deeply lobed, and the plant produces a single showy flower on each sturdy stem. The flowers are a veritable buffet for butterflies, bees, and flies, particularly when they bloom later in the season, offering an important nectar source. The abundance of insects on the flower heads is also a benefit for the birds and spiders that prey upon them. They are sometimes called brown-eyed Susans in Canada, but are not the same as the *Rudbeckia* genus. Blanketflowers are often found in commercial wildflower mixes, as they are a hardy and beautiful specimen in a naturalized garden, especially those with a xeriscape focus that relies upon little or no additional water, even in arid regions

YELLOW COLUMBINE
Aquilegia flavescens
Buttercup family (Ranunculaceae)
Quick ID: Downward-facing tubular light yellow flowers; bluish-green lobed leaves
Height: 10–28" (25–71 cm)
Bloom season: June–August

Starting in the early summer, yellow columbine makes a stunning appearance along many of the open areas along Glacier and Waterton Lakes' popular trails leading through meadows and along the forest edges. Gardeners recognize this hardy perennial, which reseeds readily, as a favorite flower in the home garden, although the domestic versions vary wildly in color and size. Each of the modified petals of the flower has a distinctive spur on the end, and the genus name *Aquilegia* is derived from the Latin word *aquila*, meaning "eagle," because the flower's spurs resemble an eagle's talons. It is a very important plant for native pollinators, including solitary bees and butterflies. At the alpine level, visitors might find the tiny but beautiful Jones' columbine (*Aquilegia jonesii*), a cushion-forming variety with blue-green foliage and purple flowers with yellow centers on short stems.

CANADA GOLDENROD
Solidago canadensis
Aster family (Asteraceae)
Quick ID: Yellow, pyramid-shaped flower heads; lance-shaped leaves
Height: 1–3' (30–91 cm)
Bloom season: July–September

The large clusters of goldenrod flowers are a familiar sight in North America, growing in every state and most Canadian provinces. Thriving from meadows to alpine regions, or even alongside the roadways, goldenrod needs sunshine. From the middle to the end of summer, look closely at the dozens of tiny flowers that create the pyramid-shaped flower head. It is an important source of pollen and nectar for butterflies, solitary bees, and beetles from midsummer up until a heavy frost. In the fall and winter, seed-eating birds utilize the remaining seeds as a food source, stashing the surplus. Canada goldenrod is known for its aggressive growth habits in some parts of the country, although it does not overcrowd its neighbors in Glacier or Waterton Lakes. Although it is often blamed for seasonal allergies, ragweeds (*Senecio* spp.) are more often the culprit.

GLACIER LILY
Erythronium grandiflorum
Lily family (Liliaceae)
Quick ID: Bright-yellow petals curl upward, and the flower has downward-facing anthers; 2 fleshy, green leaves
Height: 4–12" (4–30 cm)
Bloom season: May–August

Although there are earlier-blooming wildflowers, when the glacier lily blossoms appear, winter has finally loosened its grip. They begin in the lower elevations such as around the Goat Lick near Essex or on Going-to-the-Sun Road along McDonald Creek around Mother's Day. As the snow recedes, the yellow flower petals, which are technically tepals, curl upward. This riot of color often covers entire meadows or avalanche slopes beginning in the lower elevations early in the spring, and continuing the colorful procession as the snow melts in the higher elevations. When the flower fades, the foliage soon follows. The boardwalk at Logan Pass is sometimes closed to hiking when the glacier lilies bloom, since grizzlies frequently dig up the bulblike corms, along with the ground squirrels that live in the area that also eat them.

LANCELEAF STONECROP
Sedum lanceolatum
Stonecrop family (Crassulaceae)
Quick ID: Star-shaped, bright yellow flowers; succulent, greenish-gold pointed leaves
Height: 5–8" (12–20 cm)
Bloom season: June–August

Sedums are well adapted to the arid conditions in many areas of the region, with thick leaves that efficiently utilize the scarce moisture. Find lanceleaf stonecrop in the sunny areas along rocky outcroppings, such as near the cliff at the Pass Creek day-use area in Waterton Lakes, or among the red argillite rocks in Many Glacier. These low-growing plants have a cluster of thick leaves at the base of the plant, and the 0.5"-long (1-cm-long) foliage continues up the entire stem, at least until the plant flowers. After the flowers bloom, the leaves wither. During their brief flowering period, there are anywhere from six to over two dozen beautiful yellow blossoms, each less than 1" (2 cm) wide. The stonecrop flowers are an important resource for native pollinators because they often grow where other flowers don't.

SILKY LUPINE
Lupinus sericeus
Pea family (Fabaceae)
Quick ID: Purple/blue petals (although sometimes white); palm-shaped fuzzy leaves with 5–9 fingerlike leaflets
Height: 10–24" (25–61 cm)
Bloom season: May–July

Lupine is an easily recognizable wildflower, creating one of the first impressive botanical displays in the summer. Found in dry, sunny areas, they are prolific in meadows and open forests in the lower to mid-level elevations. The blossoms have the classic pea-flower appearance with a top banner and two identical wings below it, and while they are often found in shades of purple, there are instances when silky lupine flowers are almost white. After blooming, seedpods look like 1"-long (2-cm-long) pea pods, and usually produce up to a half-dozen seeds, which are poisonous. Although humans and most domestic livestock cannot consume any part of the plant, it is eaten by white-tailed deer and some small mammals, such as the Columbian ground squirrels that have a penchant for the flowers and leaves.

WILD BERGAMOT
Monarda fistulosa
Mint family (Lamiaceae)

Quick ID: Narrow, light purple tubular flowers radiate upward from flower head; opposite grayish-green leaves; leaves and flowers have a pleasing scent

Height: 12–24" (30–61 cm)

Bloom season: June–August

Wild bergamot, also called bee balm, is a wild relative to the often brilliant red to shades of pink varieties grown by gardeners throughout North America, who infuse it as a delicious tea or grow it to encourage pollinators. These lavender to purplish-pink flowers have a mop-top-like display perched on the long, sturdy stems. They're found in open areas, such as along the family-friendly Kootenai Brown Trail in Waterton Lakes, plus throughout higher-elevation meadows. The plants typically form a clump of foliage and spread through shallow, creeping rhizomes as well as seeds. Its square stem identifies it as a member of the mint family. With its inviting flowers and pleasing fragrance, it is an important nectar source to bees, butterflies, and hummingbirds. The seeds in the clustered heads are eaten by birds in the autumn.

ALBERTA BEARDTONGUE
Penstemon albertinus
Plantain family (Plantaginaceae)
Quick ID: Deep blue and purple tubular flowers with 2 lobes on upper lip and 3 on the bottom
Height: 4–14" (10–36 cm)
Bloom season: May–July

Penstemons are show-offs in the wildflower world, and the Alberta beardtongue delights flower lovers with its striking blossoms growing amid the rocky landscape. The flashy, tubular five-petaled flowers usually have dual shades of blue and purple, inviting bees and other pollinators to perch on the lower lip to collect pollen and nectar. The best way to watch bumblebees at work is to sit next to a patch of penstemons at this nectar-gathering hot spot. The deep-green, elongated leaves are somewhat sparse along the stems, and tend to die back after the flowers fade. Penstemons are suited for arid environments, and Alberta beardtongue is hard to miss, particularly when it is abundantly blooming in June along Going-to-the-Sun Road, as well as on the Horseshoe Basin Trail in Waterton Lakes.

LYALL'S PENSTEMON
Penstemon lyalli
Plantain family (Plantaginaceae)
Quick ID: Lavender tubular flowers; triple-lobed lower lip and double-lobed top lip on the flowers; narrow, lancelike leaves
Height: 12–28" (30–71 cm)
Bloom season: July–August

Lyall's penstemon seemingly springs forth from the gravel or sparse soil, often near streams, creating a deep green mat of sturdy foliage topped by a profusion of delicate purple flowers. While it can grow to a fair-size cluster, Lyall's penstemon does not spread quickly. Another similar variety is the rocky ledge penstemon (*Penstemon ellipticus*), but this variety is shorter and forms more of a mat-like shrub with thicker, oblong foliage, which is conducive to life in higher terrain. While the habitat of both overlaps to some degree, the rocky ledge penstemon grows at the higher elevations, and Lyall's beardtongue is not found in Waterton. With the copious blooms in the harsh and sparse reality of the subalpine reaches of the parks, both penstemons are an important resource for native bees and butterflies.

HOUNDSTONGUE
Cynoglossum officinale
Borage family (Boraginaceae)
Quick ID: Clusters of purple to reddish-purple 5-petaled flowers; large, alternate, elongated leaves; teardrop-shaped, clinging seeds
Height: 8–30" (20–76 cm)
Bloom season: May–July

Houndstongue boasts an attractive flower that resembles oblongleaf bluebells, but houndstongue is among a group of noxious weeds in Glacier and Waterton Lakes, sending down long taproots and outcompeting native vegetation. This biennial produces a rosette of large leaves with prominent veins during its first year, followed by an attractive and vigorous bloom resulting in hundreds of Velcro-like seeds that cling to hikers' socks or animals' fur, further spreading its invasive footprint. Houndstongue prefers moist, open areas and is often found in disturbed sites or where there is a fair amount of human traffic or livestock, but it is highly adaptable and can thrive in forest situations. While the flowers are beautiful, be vigilant to remove and pack out (don't toss them into the brush) any of the burrs from clothing.

OBLONGLEAF BLUEBELLS
Mertensia oblongifolia
Borage family (Boraginaceae)
Quick ID: Clusters of deep blue to purple tubular-shaped flowers that flare at the end; blue-green wide, oblong leaves
Height: 6–12" (15–30 cm)
Bloom season: June–August

Also called sagebrush bluebells, oblongleaf bluebells are found from the grasslands to mountainous terrain in open meadows and sunny areas on the edges of the forests, and are the most common of the three species found in the parks, including the rare long-flower bluebells (*Mertensia longiflora*) and the prairie bluebells (*Mertensia lanceolata*). Prairie bluebells tend to grow in the lower grasslands, where the oblong bluebells have a greater range, including mountain meadows and along streams. While all of these varieties are striking in their own right, with the beautiful hanging clusters of blue to purple flowers, sometimes with tinges of pink, bluebells are often confused for other species, such as the invasive houndstongue. The deep blue-green, smooth leaves of the penstemons are a quick giveaway that it is a different plant altogether.

LEWIS FLAX
Linum lewisii
Flax family (Linaceae)
Quick ID: 5-petaled, light purple to pale blue flowers on individual nodding stalks; tiny, narrow leaves; rounded seed capsule
Height: 12–18" (30–46 cm)
Bloom season: June–August

Lewis flax flowers are beautiful but only last for a day. Each blossom produces a round seed capsule holding ten individual seeds, growing the next year as an annual or short-lived perennial. Lewis flax shares the same growing habits and health benefits as the common flax (*Linum usitatissimum*), one of the first cultivated crops in human history. Grown to make linen as far back as 3000 BC in ancient Egypt, common flax was a prominent fiber crop until the dawn of the cotton gin. The native variety is historically utilized by indigenous people to fashion cordage for nets and other purposes, and as a nutritious addition to their diet. Elk and deer eat the semi-evergreen plants in the spring, and the seed-filled capsules are food sources for birds and small mammals.

AMERICAN VETCH
Vicia americana
Pea family (Fabaceae)
Quick ID: Climbing tendency; pealike light purple or pinkish-purple flower; compound leaves with 5–9 leaflets
Height: 1–2' (30–61 cm)
Bloom season: June–July

American vetch is an easily recognizable member of the pea family, with flowers less than 1" (2 cm) long that develop into small pea pods. While purple is the predominant color, there are variations, often with lighter colorations in the banner and wings. The leaves alternate along the stem and have tendrils at the ends to grip onto nearby vegetation, keeping the plant more upright. The deep taproot allows it to tolerate drought conditions, and like many members of the pea family, American vetch fixes nitrogen within the soil. It is highly adaptable and is found in a wide variety of terrain and growing conditions, although it is more likely seen below the alpine level. Besides being important for pollinators, elk, mule deer, black bears, and grizzlies are reported to eat the foliage and flowers.

PASQUEFLOWER
Anemone patens
Buttercup family (Ranunculaceae)
Quick ID: Blue or purple cupped flower heads made up of 6–8 petallike sepals; yellow centers; hairy, silvery leaves with 3 leaflets
Height: 4–10" (10–25 cm)
Bloom season: April–June

Early-season visitors are graced with these beautiful, early blooms that make their appearance in the spring in the lower elevations as winter loses its grip. Derived from the Greek term *pascha*, referring to Easter, pasqueflowers are connected to this spring holiday. Also called prairie crocus, particularly in Canada, they share the same tenacious characteristics as domestic crocuses, sometimes pushing through the snow to show off their 2"-wide (5-cm-wide) cup-shaped flowers. By midsummer the seeds are dispersed by a wild-looking tuft of fluff at the end of the stem reminiscent of a Dr. Seuss creation. Find pasqueflowers in meadows and open slopes from the valleys to just below the tree line, particularly on the east side in Glacier and along the Red Rock Parkway in Waterton.

BLUE CAMAS
Camassia quamash
Asparagus family (Asparagaceae)

Quick ID: Deep blue or purple, star-shaped flower heads; smooth, grasslike leaves at base of the plant

Height: 12–28" (30–70 cm)

Bloom season: May–June

The brilliant blue camas puts on a short and stunning display in fertile meadows in the lower elevations. Typically growing in large groups, they're hard to miss when they're in full bloom, with the blue or deep purple clusters of flowers resembling large stars. Deer and elk eat the foliage in the spring, while ground squirrels prefer the bulbs, sometimes stashing them in their burrows. Camas is one of the most important foods for indigenous people throughout the entire region, and has been tied into seasonal progression for generations, including digging camas bulbs when the flowers fade. This is why the June full moon is sometimes referred to as the "camas moon." Since the blue camas and all of the death camas bulbs closely resemble one another, this generational knowledge has long been critical in understanding the differences between the edible and poisonous species.

WESTERN BLUE VIRGINSBOWER
Clematis occidentalis
Buttercup family (Ranunculaceae)
Quick ID: Light to dark purple, bell-like flowers with 4 petals; each oval leaf that is pointed at the end is made up of 3 leaflets opposite along the length of the stem
Height: 2–6' (0.6–2 m)
Bloom season: April–June

In the spring and early summer look for blue virginsbower, also called purple or blue clematis, twining among the trees and shrubs in forests. While it's sometimes difficult to see the entire plant—it blends in well with other vegetation and at times grows closer to the ground, weaving itself within the low-growing plants—the large, fuzzy purple flowers hanging at eye level or climbing up the base of a tree are easy to spot. Later in the season the flowers develop into sizable, poofy seed tufts. Look for them in the valleys to slightly higher elevations on both sides of the Continental Divide, where dappled sunlight reaches the forest floor, trees, or rocky ledges.

SILKY PHACELIA
Phacelia sericea
Waterleaf family (Hydrophyllaceae)
Quick ID: Deep purple tubular flowers with yellow anthers and purple stamens protruding past the petals; fuzzy, silvery, fernlike leaves
Height: 8–16" (20–41 cm)
Bloom season: May–August

Silky phacelia seems to sparkle, showing off its brilliant purple flowers with the bright yellow anthers growing vertically in a cluster. The domestic variety, *Phacelia tanacetifolia*, is often referred to as "Bee's Friend," and this wild counterpart shares the same important qualities. One unique characteristic of silky phacelia is its role as a hyperaccumulator, a plant that pulls heavy metals from the soil, including gold (in minute levels), along with dangerous ones such as cyanide and arsenic. While this isn't an issue in the parks, experts are considering using the species for remediation in former mining sites in other regions. Preferring sunshine and being well-adapted to harsh, arid conditions, look for clusters of silky phacelia from mid-level elevations all the way to the alpine regions in talus slopes and rocky areas.

ROUNDLEAF HAREBELL
Campanula rotundifolia
Harebell family (Campanulaceae)
Quick ID: Light purple, bell-shaped flowers; stem exudes a milky sap
Height: 8–18" (20–91 cm)
Bloom season: June–September

When roundleaf harebells first emerge, they have more-rounded leaves at the base of the plant, but these die off before the light purple to deeper violet-colored flowers bloom, leaving the more-obvious longer, grasslike leaves. Sometimes referred to as bluebells, these are not the same oblong-leaf bluebells also found in the parks. The oblongleaf bluebell has deeper blue or purple flowers on top of lush, lance-shaped leaves. Often growing in clusters, roundleaf harebells are found anywhere from meadows to the base of cliffs or small meadows in the alpine realms. Yet they're so adaptable, roundleaf harebells are just as happy growing near a parking lot. With such a diverse range and long bloom time, they are a particularly important nectar and pollen source for smaller species of native bees.

STICKY JACOB'S-LADDER
Polemonium viscosum
Phlox family (Polemoniaceae)
Quick ID: Flower head with 5 lavender petals; feathery leaves
Height: 4–7" (10–18 cm)
Bloom season: July–August

Gardeners quickly recognize the classic feathery foliage with non-overlapping leaflets and bright flowers of Jacob's-ladder. This hardy alpine version, also called sky pilot, is found in scree slopes usually above the tree line. Even though it grows close to the ground, it's hard to miss in the rocky terrain. The light lavender to bright purple flowers start as a tubular shape, but gradually open to show off each petal throughout the day. Not surprising, the name references the sticky nature of its foliage, and it has an unpleasant fragrance if the leaves are crushed. The smell is fairly common in this species, as the skunkleaf Jacob's ladder (*Polemonium pulcherrimum*) also has the reputation of emitting a foul smell when its leaves are bruised. Look for the skunkleaf Jacob's ladder in lower elevations from the open foothills to the subalpine regions in similar, rocky terrain.

SPOTTED KNAPWEED
Centaurea stoebe
Aster family (Asteraceae)
Quick ID: Solitary light to bright purple rosette flowers in loose clusters; fringed leaves
Height: 6–36" (15–91 cm)
Bloom season: June–September

Although it has an attractive bachelor button–like flower and honeybees make excellent honey from its nectar, there is no doubt that spotted knapweed is an invader. Brought over from Eurasia in the 1800s, most likely in pasture seed, knapweed is notorious for overtaking large areas of grasslands. It outcompetes native plant species, poisoning the soil around them and reducing the amount of forage available to wildlife. With its long taproot, it effectively weathers fires and is difficult to pull, and even though an individual plant might only live for a few years, it produces up to four thousand seeds per plant. These remain viable for two to eight years. The seed heads are shaped like brown urns with hairlike fringe on the tops of the bracts, which persist throughout the winter.

LARKSPUR
Delphinium spp.
Buttercup family (Ranunculaceae)
Quick ID: Deep purple or blue flower heads with 5 flaring sepals; possibly a white center; spur on the back end of the top sepal; sparse leaves, mostly at the bottom
Height: 6–16" (15–40 cm)
Bloom season: April–July

As the days warm, larkspur varieties begin blooming. Not quite as early as the pasqueflower, larkspur is still one of the first flowers to appear in the meadows during the spring, creating eye-catching groups of the deep purple and sometimes blue flowers. After producing seeds, the foliage dies back for the remainder of the season. It prefers sunny areas, and is usually found in grasslands and open forests, blooming as high as the subalpine slopes later in the season. Larkspur is poisonous to cattle and people due to an alkaloid that causes paralysis and ultimately asphyxiation, although elk, mule deer, and other wildlife consume it without an issue. Larkspur varieties are very similar, mostly differing only in slight nuances of flower shape and color variations.

MOUNTAIN BOG GENTIAN
Gentiana calycosa
Gentian family (Gentianaceae)
Quick ID: Funnel-shaped, deep blue, upright flowers; elliptical leaves growing opposite each other along the stem
Height: 3–15" (7–38 cm)
Bloom season: July–September

Walking along the trails among the mountain meadows in the subalpine regions of the parks, as well as within the tree line, the bright blue flowers of the mountain bog gentian, also called explorer's gentian, are hard to miss, unless they're still closed early in the morning. Growing in groups, the 1–1.5"-long (2–3-cm-long) flowers stay tightly closed until the sun coaxes them open, revealing their pale center and bright blue petals, so it is possible to miss this shy display early in the day. While there are historical medicinal uses for aiding digestion from many of the *Gentiana* genus, all parts of the plant are poisonous. Because of its location in the subalpine regions combined with its prolific blooms and flower shape, it is an important plant for native pollinators.

ALPINE FORGET-ME-NOT
Myosotis asiatica
Borage family (Boraginaceae)
Quick ID: Tiny, blue 5-petaled flowers, often with yellow or white center; narrowly oblong, fuzzy leaves
Height: 4–8" (10–20 cm)
Bloom season: June–August

Alpine forget-me-nots are tiny, but stunning. Clusters of flat-faced, brilliant, five-petaled blue flowers, with some variations sporting a few flowers in shades of pink, are only 0.1–0.3" (4–8 mm) wide and often have yellow, or sometimes white, centers. They are clustered on top of the short stems with oblong leaves grouped at the base, although there are smaller leaves scattered along the stem. They are found in the meadows and subalpine open slopes along the upper reaches of the trails near the passes. They prefer more sun than the meadow stickseed (*Hackelia micrantha*), whose flowers look very similar to forget-me-nots, but the stickseed is much taller, doesn't grow at the upper elevations, and has prickles on the seeds that cause it to cling to fur or clothing.

INDIAN PAINTBRUSH
Castilleja spp.
Broomrape family (Orobanchaceae)
Quick ID: Red, flared-flower tops that resemble the tip of a paintbrush; lance-shaped leaves
Height: 6–24" (15–61 cm)
Bloom season: June–August

The most common Indian paintbrush varieties boast glorious shades of oranges and reds, and are some of the most photographed plants in the parks because of these brilliant colors. But there is more to this signature plant than meets the eye. The "flowers" are actually modified leaves, and while they can photosynthesize their own nutrients to some extent since they have green leaves and produce chlorophyll, they are also hemiparasitic, meaning they tap into the tissue of neighboring plants to extract water and food. With over half a dozen varieties of Indian paintbrush in Glacier and Waterton Lakes, there are a number of eye-catching red to orange colorations, such as the giant red Indian paintbrush (*Castilleja miniata*). The western Indian paintbrush (*Castilleja occidentalis*) and sulphur Indian paintbrush (*Castilleja sulphureae*) both boast light yellow blooms, and are typically found in the alpine regions.

PURPLE MONKEYFLOWER
Mimulus lewisii
Lopseed family (Phrymaceae)
Quick ID: Trumpet-shaped, hot pink/purple flowers with 5 petals and yellow streaks in the center; distinct parallel veining in the leaves
Height: 6–28" (15–71 cm)
Bloom season: June–August

Although the common name for *Mimulus lewisii* is purple monkeyflower, the color is really closer to a hot pink that screams for attention along streams and seeps. Previously grouped in the Figwort family with snapdragons, it was genetically determined to belong to a different family, although the purple monkeyflower still has a snapdragon-like appearance, with three lobes on the lower part of the petal lip and two on the top. *Mimulus* is Latin for "mimus," denoting a comical-faced actor—ideal for the whimsical appearance of the flower. This dazzling bloom is a favorite with hummingbirds and pollinating insects. Preferring wetter areas, look for it in massive groups of lush blooms, such as when hiking the Summit Lake Trail in Waterton, or in many open, moist higher-elevation areas.

MOSS CAMPION
Silene acaulis
Pink family (Caryophyllaceae)
Quick ID: 5-petaled pink flowers; thick mats of tiny, lancelike, evergreen leaves
Height: 1–4" (2–10 cm)
Bloom season: July–August

Moss campion is one of those extraordinarily tough alpine plants that grow with little or no soil, in regions where snow hangs on until late into the summer, and brutally desiccating winds force it to efficiently utilize what little moisture is available. Despite these conditions, moss campion forms a cushion of beautiful pink blooms, creating a dense mat up to 18" (46 cm) in diameter. It's considered an eco-nursery plant because this long-growing plant, often over a century old, provides other alpine species a way to take hold. It's also critical for the bees that inhabit this region. Look for moss campion in the rugged areas of the high country near the passes in Glacier, as well as along Akamina Ridge in Waterton Lakes, where it blooms in mid- to late summer before the snow starts again.

ELEPHANTHEAD LOUSEWORT
Pedicularis groenlandica
Broomrape family (Orobanchaceae)
Quick ID: Bright pink flower resembling the head of an elephant; fernlike 2–6"-long (4–12-cm-long) leaves
Height: 4–26" (10–66 cm)
Bloom season: July–August

With a name like elephanthead, it's worth taking a closer look at this unique plant, with the frontal tube of its flower resembling the upwardly turned trunk of an elephant, and the two identical lobes flaring out on the side like the elephant's ears. These miniature, hot pink pachyderms march up the stem, retaining their unique shape even after going to seed. Growing in colorful groups from the mid-elevation mountainous regions to alpine wetlands and along streams, they are often found where sedges grow in the subalpine regions. Like the Indian paintbrushes, elephant-head lousewort is a hemiparasitic plant. It produces some chlorophyll on its own, but taps into the roots of neighboring plants for nutrients and water and to obtain anything else it requires in this harsh environment.

PRAIRIE SMOKE
Geum triflorum
Rose family (Rosaceae)
Quick ID: Reddish-pink, nodding, bell-shaped flowers; fernlike gray-green leaves; flower heads turn into feathery, pink seed heads after fertilization
Height: 12–15" (30–38 cm)
Bloom season: April–June

This early-spring flower makes a beautiful display, growing in groups in the grasslands and on southerly, exposed slopes, particularly prolific in the lower-elevation meadows. Since prairie smoke blooms shortly after the snow leaves, it's an important source of food for bumblebees when they emerge, as well as an attractant to butterflies and other native bees in the early summer. After fertilization, it's obvious why prairie smoke picked up its other common name, old man's whiskers, because the once-nodding bell-shaped flowers turn upward and form a feathery plume with the uncanny appearance of a fluffy beard. In large groups, the landscape takes on a pinkish tone. Even the foliage is unique, turning reddish in the autumn and holding on to a red-purple color into the winter.

DARKTHROAT SHOOTING STAR
Primula pauciflora
Primrose family (Primulaceae)
Quick ID: Downward-facing flower with magenta petals and yellow center; oblong leaves clustered at the base
Height: 4–12" (10–30 cm)
Bloom season: May–August

Shooting stars have a well-deserved name, as every flower looks like a miniature celestial celebration with several small but dazzling magenta blossoms. The backward-flaring petals show off the yellow center pointing downward from the corolla like a beak on the slender, leafless, sometimes maroon-colored stem. The leaves typically die back after the plants finish flowering. Look for them early in the season in the valleys, but don't be surprised to find them blooming in the middle of the summer at higher elevations. Shooting stars prefer moist areas, such as along streambanks, near waterfalls, or even interspersed in wet meadows, growing in small colonies in either sun or partial shade. Bumblebees are attracted to the bright blossoms, and sometimes deer, elk, and small mammals browse upon the leaves and flowers early in the season.

STICKY GERANIUM
Geranium viscosissimum
Geranium family (Geraniaceae)
Quick ID: Pink, saucer-shaped flower; palmated leaves; sticky to the touch
Height: 1–3' (30–91 cm)
Bloom season: May–August

Sticky geraniums are one of those flowers that put on a show through-out a good portion of the summer in a wide variety of habitats. Found in grasslands, forests, or wetter habitats in full sun to partial shade, the beau-tiful pink 1–1.5"-wide (2–3-cm-wide) flowers attract bumblebees and other pollinators, but sometimes the insects become food for the plant. If a small fly or other type of tiny insect is trapped upon the sticky surface, the geranium dissolves it, utilizing the nitrogen from the protein. The leaves are eaten by elk, deer, and grazing bears. The seed capsules, which resemble a crane's bill, produce seeds that are important to rodents and birds. Look for them in the grasslands along the Red Rock Parkway, as well as in the open areas of Two Medicine, St. Mary, and Many Glacier.

PINK WINTERGREEN
Pyrola asarifolia
Heath family (Ericaceae)
Quick ID: Small, nodding, pink flowers; deep green, glossy foliage
Height: 8–16" (20–41 cm)
Bloom season: June–August

Found in denser forests, often near streams or other water sources, the dainty five-petaled light-pink flowers bloom atop the single stems of the pink wintergreen. They are particularly eye-catching against the dark roundish or heart-shaped evergreen leaves, and grow from the lower elevations to as high as the subalpine regions. Pink wintergreen has a beneficial relationship with the mycorrhizal fungi within the soil system. While the plant has leaves and can fix carbon through photosynthesis to some degree, it is partially mycoheterotrophic, meaning it also depends upon the fungi surrounding the roots of vascular plants, such as nearby trees, for the carbohydrates they make through photosynthesis. By utilizing this network, the pink wintergreen absorbs nutrients it can't produce. It primarily spreads through shallow rhizomes, although also creates dust-speck–size seeds, which grow with the help of the soil fungi.

FIREWEED
Chamerion angustifolium
Evening Primrose family (Onagraceae)
Quick ID: Rosy-pink 4-petaled flowers on extended clusters; narrow leaves
Height: 3–9' (0.9–3 m)
Bloom season: June–September

Fireweed earns its name due to its tendency to colonize areas after wild-fires. The fluff-ended seeds are found in four-chambered 1–4"-long (2–10-cm-long) capsules, and each plant produces up to eighty thousand seeds that are carried away on the wind. They also spread via rhizomes that stretch throughout the soil. There is a grand display along the Red Rock Parkway after the 2017 Kenow Wildfire in Waterton Lakes. Although they are prolific in newly opened areas, the large groups of fireweed are succeeded by trees and thicker understory plants as the forest rebounds. Fireweed is an excellent nectar plant for bees. Elk, deer, and grizzlies also feed upon the early-spring plants. Found in gravelly areas near streams and rivers or in the higher elevations, dwarf fireweed (*Chamerion latifolium*) is shorter, with bluish-green leaves and larger, but fewer, flowers.

GREEN FALSE HELLEBORE
Veratrum viride
Bunchflower family (Melanthiaceae)
Quick ID: Pale green flowers; large parallel veined leaves up to 15" (38 cm) long
Height: 2–7' (0.5–2 m)
Bloom season: June–July

It is common to have meadows and open forested trails, particularly where there is persistent water, lined with this majestic, lush green plant, but leave it alone, as false hellebore is very poisonous. In the same family as death camas—not the hellebores from the home garden—it contains over fifty alkaloids, and is reported to slow the heart, lower blood pressure to dangerous levels, and inhibit breathing, along with a number of violent gastrointestinal symptoms. If there is any ingestion, even in small quantities, seek medical help immediately. From the moment it curls out of the earth in early spring, the leaves are large and striking, and while the six-petaled green flowers are not showy, nor do they typically form until the plant is approximately ten years old, this is a plant that is hard to miss.

STINGING NETTLE
Urtica dioica
Nettle family (Urticaceae)
Quick ID: Tiny, green flowers on axils of upper leaves; leaves have serrated edges and are pointed at the end
Height: 2–5' (0.5–1.5 m)
Bloom season: June–July

Stinging nettle is an unremarkable-looking plant usually growing in patches along the trails in moist meadows or open forests, but it quickly gains attention if it is accidentally touched. Hollow hairs on the leaves inject histamines, formic acid, and several other chemical compounds into whatever, or whomever, brushes up against it. The result is a sharp stinging pain that sometimes results in a burning rash. Each plant produces either male or female flowers, which are utilized as food sources for butterflies and other pollinators. The female plants create thousands of seeds that are eaten by birds and small mammals. Historically, nettles were used to make cordage for nets (hence, the name), and it is well-known for its nutritional value, including vitamin C. Fortunately, the stinging quality goes away when it's cooked.

GRIZZLY BEAR
Ursus arctos
Bear family (Ursidae)
Quick ID: Blond to dark brown with silver tips on the fur; dished face; rounded ears; distinct muscular shoulder hump; 2–4" (5–10 cm), often visible, claws
Length: 4–6' (1–2 m)
Weight: 250–600 lbs (113–272 kg)

Despite their impressive size and unwarranted ferocious reputation, grizzlies are the ultimate omnivore. Early greens, roots, bulbs, and winter-killed carrion are their primary focus when they emerge from their dens in March and April. Females give birth over the winter and emerge with cubs in the spring. Their sense of smell, which is reportedly seven times stronger than a bloodhound's, leads them to berry patches or unsuspecting ground squirrels in their burrows. This push for food is so strong, some grizzlies climb high peaks to consume the fat-rich army cutworm moths spending the days below the boulders and talus. Watching a grizzly is a memorable experience, but it is best done from a safe distance of at least 100 yards (100 m).

BLACK BEAR
Ursus americanus
Bear family (Ursidae)
Quick ID: Black, shades of brown, blond, and cinnamon colorations; straight muzzle; taller, less-rounded ears
Length: 60–71" (150–180 cm)
Weight: 120–250 lbs (54–113 kg)

Black bears are often confused with grizzlies due to their individual coat variations, making it important to look beyond color. Besides the straighter facial profile, black bears lack the muscular hump over their front shoulders, although it sometimes requires careful observation, especially when they are fat and furry at the end of the season. Each female has one to three cubs that stay with her for two seasons. She will send them up a tree in the case of danger, sometimes following them. They are proficient omnivores, feeding on vegetation as soon as they emerge from their dens, often a burrow under rocks or in a hollow tree, and, like grizzlies, food is their focus throughout the season. Serviceberries and chokecherries are summer favorites, along with juniper, mountain ash, and kinni-kinnick berries in the fall. Even though they appear docile, always give them at least 100 yards (100 m) of space.

Kari Cieszkiewicz, USFWS

WOLF
Canis lupus
Dog family (Canidae)
Quick ID: Black, mixes of gray and white, sometimes with brown markings on face or underbelly; long legs; bushy tail nearly one-third of the length of their body; tapered snout
Length: 70–73" (180–186 cm)
Weight: 80–104 lbs (36–47 kg)

Extirpated from Montana in the 1930s, a few wolves traveled from British Columbia into Glacier and the surrounding areas by the 1970s. With an average of seven wolves in a pack—although it's more likely to only see one or two at a time—sightings are hit-and-miss throughout the parks. Opportunistic carnivores, they pursue anything from rodents to moose, and will push mountain lions or coyotes off a carcass, even if they didn't kill the animal. While coyotes are often mistaken for wolves, particularly since young wolves might resemble an adult coyote, they are easily differentiated, as adult wolves stand taller and move with an easy, gliding gait. Tracks typically measure 3.75–5.75" (9.5–15 cm). They are often heard more than they are seen, with deeper and more-drawn-out howls than the higher-pitched call, often punctuated by yips, of the coyote.

COYOTE
Canis latrans
Dog family (Canidae)

Quick ID: Gray or reddish-gray; reddish-brown on legs; white on throat and belly area; bushy tail; pointy nose and ears; narrow snout; similar in size to a medium-size dog
Length: 44–48" (113–122 cm)
Weight: 22–28 lbs (10–13 kg)

Although they are most often viewed in open meadows and clearings, coyotes travel throughout the lower-elevation landscapes in search of a meal, which is anything from carrion to voles, ground squirrels, or deer, whether fawns in the spring or adults in the winter. They'll eat insects, such as grasshoppers, as well as berries or other vegetation. Coyotes mate for life, averaging four to seven pups each season. Their dens are found under tree roots, rocks, or dug out in a bank, and both parents equally care for the young until they venture out on their own between six and nine months of age. Their calls are heard at night as a combination of high-pitched howls, barks, and yips to communicate with their pack mates.

Evgeny555 / iStock / Getty Images Plus

MOUNTAIN LION
Puma concolor
Cat family (Felidae)
Quick ID: Tan to beige, sometimes silvery gray; white fur on underbelly, chest, and often around the mouth; short, rounded ears; long tail tipped in black
Length: 59–107" (150–273 cm)
Weight: 70–190 lbs (31–86 kg)

Stealthy and secretive, mountain lions (also called cougars) are found where there is cover and prey, equally at home in forests, river bottoms, rocky outcroppings, and even near populated areas. With large, front-set eyes and a lithe, powerful body, they are exceptional ambush predators, hunting everything from rodents to moose. Mountain lions are solitary animals, with the exception of a female with kittens, who remain with her until they are nearly two years old. One of their most surprising characteristics is the high-pitched, chirping call between females and their young. While mountain lion attacks are rare, if one is encountered, watch the cat, and slowly move out of the area. If the lion shows interest, appear as big as possible to discourage an encounter. Fight, if necessary. Bear spray is also effective.

MikeLane45 / iStock / Getty Images Plus

CANADA LYNX
Lynx canadensis
Cat family (Felidae)
Quick ID: Silvery-gray to graying brown; white on throat; ruff around face; tufted ears with black on tips; short tail with black tip
Length: 30–35" (70–89 cm)
Weight: 15–35 lbs (7–16 kg)

Strong and stealthy, lynxes are well suited to their home in boreal spruce-fir forests, where the deep snow allows them to travel quietly while hunting their preferred prey, the snowshoe hare. Like the hare, lynxes are equally equipped with large, fur-covered paws that act as snowshoes in the deep powder. They thrive during long winters with heavy snow because it reduces the success of other predators who target the same species. When hares aren't prolific, they rely on squirrels, grouse, and other small game, plus they take advantage of carrion. Breeding occurs in April and May, with three to four kittens born in the summer. This might only occur every other year depending on the hare population. The kittens stay with the mother for nearly a year.

twildlife / iStock / Getty Images Plus

BOBCAT
Lynx rufus
Cat family (Felidae)
Quick ID: Shades of yellowish- or reddish-brown; brown or black spots; small tufts of hair on the tips of the ears; black on the back of the ear with a white spot; bobbed tail with black tip
Length: 28–37" (71–94 cm)
Weight: 11–35 lbs (5–16 kg)

Bobcats and lynx are similar in appearance, although the end of a bobcat's tail is darker on top and lighter underneath, plus its ears and feet are smaller. Because bobcats do not have the snowshoe-like qualities of the lynx, they prefer a landscape with less deep snow. Bobcats seek cottontail rabbits and snowshoe hares, but will kill small birds, rodents, frogs, and even deer. They are active in the late afternoon to nearly midnight and then again around sunrise. Solitary except during breeding in February or March, or when rearing their two to four kittens for approximately a year, territories are marked by a scrape incorporating urine, feces, and excretions from their anal gland to let other bobcats know to find their own space.

RED FOX
Vulpes vulpes
Dog family (Canidae)
Quick ID: Reddish coat; sometimes with a dark cross fur pattern on its back and shoulders; tall, pointed ears; bushy tail with white tip
Length: 39–43" (99–110 cm)
Weight: 10–15 lbs (5–7 kg)

Although they hunt more at night, foxes that are seen during the day, traveling through or along the edge of a meadow or forest, are typically on a mission to catch rodents, eat eggs, snag a frog, or find a carrion meal. They use their exceptional hearing to pinpoint the movement of their prey beneath the grass or snow, and pounce on an unsuspecting mouse or vole underneath their seemingly protective cover. Foxes dig out dens in the spring in a bank or in a meadow, and once the pups are old enough to venture outside, they are a treat to watch (from a distance) as they play and practice their skills while the parents hunt. Foxes have a wide variety of vocalizations ranging from a *yow, yow, yow* to a sharp bark, or a spine-chilling yowl that sounds like a woman's scream.

Erik Peterson, Glacier NPS

WOLVERINE
Gulo gulo
Weasel family (Mustelidae)
Quick ID: Low, thick body; dark fur with light band along the side; white or lighter fur around the throat and chest; large paws with visible claws; bushy tail
Length: 35–43" (90–110 cm)
Weight: 15–55 lbs (7–25kg)

It's a once-in-a-lifetime experience to see a wolverine in the wild, and although it's never a sure thing, the possibility exists throughout the subalpine to alpine regions in both parks. With a loping, arching gait, they resemble a combination of bear and badger. A female has a litter of six to nine kits in the winter, which stay with her until they disperse on their own in the fall. Renowned for their fierce personality, they are equally opportunistic, indicated by their name, *gulo*, meaning "glutton" in Latin. They'll eat anything and everything from berries to fish, eggs, marmots, and even mountain goats, and are known to push other carnivores, including grizzlies, off a carcass. What a wolverine wants, a wolverine gets.

ELK
Cervus canadensis
Deer family (Cervidae)
Quick ID: Tawny brown with a light rump; dark around legs, head, and neck; bulls have impressive antlers
Length: 6.5–8' (2–2.5 m)
Weight: 500–900 lbs (227–408 kg)

During the warmer months, elk head for higher terrain, but as the days chill, they are more visible in the valleys. Elk prefer open areas surrounded by the protection of timber, such as lodgepole or ponderosa pines and aspen groves, which are used particularly in the winter when the snow is deep, as they browse on the twigs, new shoots, and bark. They're often spotted at Two Dog Flats near St. Mary, in the North Fork, among the slopes of the southern boundary visible from US 2, as well as in the valley around Waterton Lakes. Calves are born in May and June. Give a cow more than the required 25 yards (30 m) of distance even if a calf isn't readily seen. Beginning in the early spring, the bulls sport new, velvety antler growth, but the real show is during the rut in September, when their piercing bugling challenges rivals, sometimes resulting in dramatic fights.

WHITE-TAILED DEER

Odocoileus virginianus
Deer family (Cervidae)

Quick ID: Reddish-brown to gray; white on underside, including below the throat and under the tail; bucks have antlers with a main beam pointing forward

Length: 4–7' (1–2 m)
Weight: 160–275 lbs (72–125 kg)

Traveling through river- and creek-bottom corridors, or areas with dense vegetation to provide cover and feed, whitetails thrive in a variety of terrain. They're seen around West Glacier and Apgar, in the North Fork area, and among the aspen groves in Waterton Lakes. Breeding occurs in the fall, with the peak of the rut around mid-November, resulting in one to two fawns the following spring. Even though they may seem docile, stay at least 25 yards (30 m) away from deer, particularly does in the early summer, and never feed them, as they become habituated and aggressive. Whitetails are primarily browsers that eat the twigs of serviceberries, chokecherries, and dogwoods, as well as conifers during the winter. Since they are a prey species to many carnivores, they are always wary, and a common sight is their white tail waving as they dash away.

MULE DEER
Odocoileus hemionus
Deer family (Cervidae)
Quick ID: Brown coat that tends to turn grayish in the winter; dark patch on forehead; white on throat and rump; white tail with black tip; large ears; bucks have upright forked antlers
Length: 4–7' (1–2 m)
Weight: 160–275 lbs (72–125 kg)

The large ears of the mule deer are an easy way to identify them, and sharp hearing allows them to pinpoint potential predators, inspiring them to flee using a vertical bouncing motion with all four feet held together, called stotting. Found in the foothills from coulees to river bottoms, or as high as the subalpine regions of both parks, mule deer thrive anywhere there is cover and feed. Focusing on shrubby browse such as serviceberries, along with herbaceous plants, they are plentiful in Waterton Lakes, where it's not unusual to see them helping themselves to the delicious landscaping within the townsite. Be particularly wary when town does have fawns. Bucks posture and fight in November for breeding rights, shedding their antlers in January and February.

MOUNTAIN GOAT
Oreamnos americanus
Cattle family (Bovidae)
Quick ID: Pure white coats; white beard on both sexes; 8–10" (20–25 cm) dark horns curve backward (on males and females)
Length: 3–5' (91–152 cm)
Weight: 120–300 lbs (54–136 kg)

Alongside the grizzly, the mountain goat is a symbol of Glacier. They call the highest peaks home, although the salt from human hands on railings, or bathroom breaks on the trails, along with the reduced predator pressure around humans, is appealing enough to keep them near the crowds at Logan Pass and some backcountry campgrounds. Even when they're close, do your best to stay 25 yards (30 m) away. Absolutely do not feed or pet them. Mountain goats are some of the best adapted animals for this frozen realm, with a thick, double coat making them impervious to temperatures dipping to -50 F (-45 C), with winds often over 100 mph (161 km/h). The soft pads on their specialized hooves allow them to navigate sheer cliffs with amazing ease. An excellent opportunity to view their dexterity is at the Goat Lick along US 2 near Essex in the early summer.

BIGHORN SHEEP
Ovis canadensis
Cattle family (Bovidae)
Quick ID: Brownish-gray bodies; white on rump; white around nose and mouth; short brown tail; males (rams) have large curled horns; females (ewes) have shorter horns that sweep backward
Length: 4.5–6' (137–182 cm)
Weight: 120–350 lbs (54–159 kg)

During the early summer and again in the fall, bighorn sheep, particularly the ewes, remain in the lower elevations of Many Glacier, Two Medicine, and often in the Waterton Lakes townsite. Although they appear tame, stay at least 25 yards (30 m) away from them, even when they don't follow the same guideline. As the weather warms, bighorn sheep head to the high country, with the ewes and lambs staying together while the rams gather in bachelor groups. They are often seen at this time along the Highline Trail, the Grinnell Trail, and on the slopes leading to Ptarmigan Tunnel. Forage consists of grasses, herbaceous plants, sedges in the summer, and browsing on shrubs during the winter. The rut in November is dramatic, with rams bashing into each other's heads at full speed, resulting in one lamb born in April and May.

AMERICAN BISON
Bison bison
Cattle family (Bovidae)
Quick ID: Brown to dark brown fur, curly toward the shoulder and front end; massive head; hump on the shoulder; curved dark horns
Length: 7–12' (2–3.6 m)
Weight: 700–2,000 lbs (318–907 kg)

Before the 1500s, an estimated sixty million bison roamed throughout North America. Their decline due to economic motivation, hunting pressure, and the political expediency of controlling the indigenous people, pushed the population to near extirpation in 1870s. With keen senses of smell, hearing, and sight, plus amazing quickness—they can run 38 mph (62 km/h)—they are well-suited to live with their main predators, wolves and mountain lions. Bulls vie for breeding rights in mid-July to the end of August, resulting in a single calf approximately nine months later. Calves are on their feet within hours of birth, and stay with their mother for a year. In 1952, Waterton created the bison paddock at the northern border of the park along AB 6 to maintain a representation of these majestic animals that once roamed freely in the area. The Blackfeet Nation also has a herd near East Glacier, outside of the park, that is visible from US 2 during the summer.

MOOSE
Alces alces
Deer family (Cervidae)
Quick ID: Up to 6' (1.5 m) tall at the shoulder; dark coat; "bell" of skin hangs from the throat; bulbous overhanging muzzle; bulls have palmated antlers
Length: 7–10' (2–3 m)
Weight: 600–1,000 lbs (272–454 kg)

Glacier and Waterton Lakes National Parks are home to the Shiras subspecies, the smallest, yet still impressive, member of the moose family. Primarily browsers of submerged water plants and herbaceous plants in the summer, plus willows, birch, and aspen trees in the winter, moose are found near water throughout both parks. While feeding within the water, they can keep their head submerged for several minutes at a time by closing their nostrils. Mating takes place toward the end of September and into October, resulting in one to two calves born in May or June. While they look relaxed and slow, they can flip from docile to aggressive in a nanosecond, and one of the most terrifying and dangerous sights is a protective cow moose. Avoid being too close at any time of the year, staying at least 25 yards (30 m) away.

HOARY MARMOT
Marmota caligata
Squirrel family (Sciuridae)
Quick ID: Grizzled gray fur; short and stocky; dark paws; long tail
Length: 22–28" (56–72 cm)
Weight: 13–25 lbs (6–11 kg)

Residents of the subalpine and alpine regions, hoary marmots often greet travelers with a resonating whistle, alerting members of their family-based colony—and everyone else in the area. Looking like very large versions of ground squirrels, they have litters of two to four pups every other year, and the young stay with the colony for a couple of seasons before dispersing to their own territory. Their favorite places are in the high parks of the subalpine terrain, where the soil is soft enough to make a burrow, yet close to boulder fields or talus slopes to find the perfect sunning rocks. Young marmots are a delight to watch, as they'll often wrestle and chase each other through the rocky alpine landscape. Throughout the short summers, they eat enough vegetation to put on nearly half their body weight in fat reserves for their long winter hibernation, typically lasting from September to May.

PIKA
Ochotona princeps
Pika family (Ochotonidae)
Quick ID: Thick fur; light brown, sometimes tinged with gray; rounded ears; oval-shaped body
Length: 6–8" (15–20 cm)
Weight: 4–6 oz (113–170 g)

Living above 5,600' (1,707 m), these small, rabbit-like bundles of cuteness thrive in boulder fields and talus slopes in the alpine regions. With a body temperature of 104 degrees F (40 C), external temperatures below 80 degrees F (26 C) are critical, as they suffer heat exhaustion unless they are able to find a cool shelter beneath the rocks. As a result, they are keenly affected by the changing climate. Pika do not hibernate, so they spend the summer gathering grasses and herbaceous plants, creating "hay" piles to consume throughout the winter, some of which may be over 2' (61 cm) in diameter. They are most visible while creating these caches, dashing over and in between rocks. The easiest way to find them is to listen for their distinctive *eep* sound, stop and scan the rocky terrain for movement, then sit back and watch them work.

Glacier NPS

NORTH AMERICAN RIVER OTTER
Lontra canadensis
Weasel family (Mustelidae)
Quick ID: Dark brown, thick coat; long, powerful tail; small, rounded ears; oval head
Length: 35–53" (89–135 cm)
Weight: 20–33 lbs (9–15 kg)

River otters are powerful swimmers with specialized webbed feet on their short legs, diving to 45' (14 m) deep, and they have the ability to spend nearly four minutes underwater. With a thick undercoat to keep them warm, along with guard hairs that do not freeze, they are perfectly adapted to the cold waters of this region. Otters are typically spotted in the swift-running streams and rivers, as well as cruising lakes in search of crayfish, fish, turtles, frogs, and aquatic plants. They are equally proficient on land, moving between water sources traveling in pairs or family groups, with the mother and two to three pups. Otters exhibit playful behavior and spend a considerable amount of time grooming their coats. Despite their cuteness, they are aggressive when defending their young, and have attacked swimmers and boaters. Give them a wide berth.

SHORT-TAILED WEASEL
Mustela erminea
Weasel family (Mustelidae)
Quick ID: Slender body; brown fur on the top with creamy fur underneath
Length: 7–13" (18–33 cm)
Weight: 1–6 oz (28–170 g)

There are two other weasel species in the parks besides the short-tailed weasel, including the long-tailed weasel (*Mustela frenata*) and the least weasel (*Mustela nivalis*). All three have brown fur on their uppersides, are cream-colored underneath, including the throat, and turn white in the winter. The long- and short-tailed weasels will eat anything from eggs and mice to birds or rabbits, while least weasels prey primarily on mice, sometimes pursuing them into their holes. The short-tailed weasel is smaller, with a shorter tail and a quick, hopping motion, but they, as well as the long-tailed weasels, retain the black tip on their tails in the winter. The least weasel is the smallest of the trio, weighing only 1–3 oz (28–85 g). It has a similar coloration pattern, although it loses the black tip on its tail during the winter, except for possibly a few remnant dark hairs.

PORCUPINE
Erethizon dorsatum
Porcupine family (Erethizontidae)
Quick ID: Covered in brown or light-colored quills over a brownish undercoat; round body;
long claws; slow-moving
Length: 25–36" (64–91 cm)
Weight: 12–30 lbs (5–14 kg)

Although their native range is throughout the region, porcupines are more often found east of the Continental Divide, as their population declines, due to unknown reasons, in the western forests. Porcupines are not speedy characters, but what they lack in fast motion they make up for in superior defensive mechanisms, with up to thirty thousand 5" (13 cm) quills armoring their bodies. Porcupines are generally docile, but when danger is close, they are quick to defend themselves by flicking their tail at the threat. They climb trees to eat the twigs and the bark, along with consuming grasses and other vegetation throughout the season. Porcupines will also chew on sweaty hiking boots and backpacks, sometimes gnawing through the straps. This makes it very important to secure all of your camp gear out of their reach.

Glacier NPS

BEAVER
Castor canadensis
Beaver family (Castoridae)
Quick ID: Slick dark fur; large bodies, large paddle-like, scale-covered tail; large incisors
Length: 35–54" (89–137 cm)
Weight: 35–65 lbs (16–29 kg)

Beavers are the largest rodents in North America, renowned for their engineering skills in reshaping the landscape. Generally monogamous, family groups chew down willows, cottonwoods, and aspens near their water source to build dams and a lodge, and to feed their young, consuming roughly two hundred small trees per year. Since they don't hibernate, if trees are chewed several feet (or a meter or more) up the trunk, it's most likely due to them working while standing on the deep snow. Beavers are most often viewed around dawn or dusk, and will sound an alarm to others by smacking their large tail on the water before disappearing below the surface in a blink. They can remain submerged for up to fifteen minutes, and their eyes have a transparent covering that allows them to see beneath the surface.

MUSKRAT
Ondatra zibethicus
Mice, Rat, and Vole family (Cricetidae)
Quick ID: Dark brown, sleek fur; stocky body; long hairless tail
Length: 16–26" (41–66 cm)
Weight: 2–4 lbs (1–2 kg)

Muskrats live in a similar habitat as beavers, although they are equally suited to shallower marshes and ponds. Congregating in family groups, muskrats burrow into the banks, or in a situation where there are no steep banks, they'll construct dome-like dens out of mud, reeds, and other vegetation, with the entrance above the waterline. While muskrats look similar to beavers—albeit, much smaller, with a thinner, almost rat-like tail—they are unrelated. Even so, both are proficient swimmers and can spend considerable time underwater. Muskrats prefer cattails and other herbaceous vegetation, although they will also eat small birds, fish, and mussels, consuming close to one-third of their body weight every day. Look for muddy trails in the water leading away from the bank, and although they are primarily nocturnal, it's not uncommon to spot a musk-rat cruising through the water in the afternoon or early evening.

SNOWSHOE HARE
Lepus americanus
Rabbit family (Leporidae)
Quick ID: Light brown with a white undercoat during the summer; winter coat is white; long ears; large feet
Length: 16–20" (41–51cm)
Weight: 2–4 lbs (1–2 kg)

As implied by their name, snowshoe hares rely on their 6"-long (15-cm-long) feet covered in fur to help them run on top of the snow, because their life literally depends upon it. Hares are the preferred prey species for owls, coyotes, and foxes, and are particularly important to lynx. Their seasonal color change helps them avoid predators, but when pursued, they can top speeds of 27 mph (43 km/h), cover 10' (3 m) in a single jump, and are masters at dodging and darting away from predators. Living in the forests, hares consume twigs, bark, and herbaceous plants, plus they depend upon spruce needles during the winter. Because they can't digest these high-fiber foods in a single process, they routinely eat their feces, called coprophagy, further utilizing nutrients from predigested matter.

MOUNTAIN COTTONTAIL
Sylvilagus nuttallii
Rabbit family (Leporidae)
Quick ID: Brownish-gray; light gray to white on the belly; large tail looks like a cotton ball; large eyes; shorter, rounded ears
Length: 13–16" (33–41 cm)
Weight: 1–2 lbs (0.5–1 kg)

Cottontails prefer living on the outskirts of forests or in open meadows to be near cover, since they are on the menu for raptors, coyotes, and bobcats. Relying on their coloration to blend into their surroundings, keeping absolutely still to avoid detection, they sprint away to find cover if danger gets too close. They feed primarily in the early mornings and late afternoons, focusing on grasses and leafy plants. In the winter, cottontails browse on twigs and bark sticking out above the snow. Breeding takes place from March to July, and after a monthlong gestation period, the female usually has two to four kits that are on their own within a month. They can have multiple litters each year, with females breeding as early as three months old.

COLUMBIAN GROUND SQUIRREL
Urocitellus columbianus
Squirrel family (Sciuridae)
Quick ID: Mottled grayish-brown body; light underbelly; 3–5"-long (8–13 cm-long) bushy tail; small, rounded ears
Length: 10–12" (25–30 cm)
Weight: 11–28 oz (312–794 g)

Found from the valleys to the open alpine meadows, Columbian ground squirrels rely on each other to watch for predators, sounding the alarm by standing erect and giving out a loud squeak before diving back into their burrows. They're very visible, begging at lodges, visitor centers, and trails, but do not feed them. Left to their natural diet, they prefer grasses, herbaceous plants, fruits, seeds, and the bulblike corms of glacier lilies. Their propensity for this important food source also places them in an undesirable position, as grizzlies excavate the ground squirrels for a protein-rich meal along with the glacier lilies. In reality, most predators have ground squirrels on their menu. While the ground squirrels feed voraciously during the brief summer, they hibernate as soon as their food sources fade, sometimes as early as August.

GOLDEN-MANTLED GROUND SQUIRREL
Callospermophilus lateralis
Squirrel family (Sciuridae)
Quick ID: Brownish-gray body; russet around shoulders and on head; black stripes with white on either side of central stripe; white around eyes
Length: 9–12" (23–30 cm)
Weight: 4–14 oz (113–397 g)

The golden-mantled ground squirrel tends to resemble a large chipmunk, yet its size and tendency to beg from hikers gives it away as a fellow ground squirrel. Do not feed them, as it's healthier for them to rely on natural foods such as herbaceous plants, insects, fungi, and even carrion, along with the typical seeds and fruits, in order to put on enough fat to hibernate through the winter. They do not form colonies like other ground squirrels, so they don't often chirp or squeak as an alarm. The golden-mantled ground squirrels are found throughout the parks in conifer forests and as high up as the timberline, often in the remnants of limber bark pine stands, where they burrow under the old roots.

RED SQUIRREL
Tamiasciurus hudsonicus
Squirrel family (Sciuridae)
Quick ID: Reddish-brown or gray on the back; light cream or white underbelly; gray to red tail with a black stripe the entire length
Length: 10–15" (25–38 cm)
Weight: 7–10 oz (192–282 g)

It can be difficult to hike through the coniferous forest, particularly at the lower elevations, without being called out by a red squirrel. Highly territorial, they alert the entire area with a variety of rattles, screeches, chirps, or barks, letting intruders know that they are on their radar. Throughout the year, red squirrels busily cache food in mounds called middens, which include a variety of fungi and pinecones. They will also eat tree buds and bark, and sometimes even insects and small bird eggs. They are an important part of the forest ecosystem, as they disperse fungi when they excavate them, as well as inadvertently providing a nutrition resource for bears who take advantage of the stashed food piles.

Ann Froschauer, USFWS

LITTLE BROWN BAT
Myotis lucifugus
Evening Bats family (Vespertilionidae)
Quick ID: Light to dark brown with lighter underbelly; large, dark brown ears; practically hairless brown wing membranes
Length: 2–4" (5–10 cm)
Weight: 0.2–0.5 oz (6–14 g)

One of the most common bats in North America, the little brown bat is an insect-eating powerhouse. Feeding mostly after dusk and before sunrise, each bat consumes up to 1,200 insects each night. In between feedings, they roost in the tiniest crevices within the cracks of tree bark, in openings of cliffs or rocky outcroppings, as well as behind the siding of some of the parks' buildings. As the weather chills in the early fall, they congregate in hibernacula where the temperature stays above freezing in order to remain in a type of a hibernation mode, where their heart rate slows to ten to twenty beats per minute. Little brown bats are vulnerable to predators such as owls, weasels, and mink, as well as the fungal disease called white nose syndrome, which has affected populations in the eastern part of North America.

References

Arora, D. *Mushrooms Demystified*, 2nd ed. Berkley, CA: Ten Speed Press, 1986.

Benson, D. *Glacier Is for the Birds: A Trail Guide to the Birds of Glacier National Park*, 2nd ed. Indianapolis, IN: Habitats for All Press, 2016.

Elbroch, M. *Mammal Track & Sign: A Guide to North American Species.* Mechanicsburg, PA: Stackpole Books, 2003.

Hart, J. *Montana Native Plants & Early Peoples.* Helena: Montana Historical Society Press, 2007.

Jarrand, J. *An Audubon Handbook: Western Birds.* New York: Chanticleer Press, Inc., 1988.

Lesica, P. *Flora of Glacier National Park.* Corvallis: Oregon State University Press, 2002.

Lesica, P., and S. Fitzpatrick Kimball. *Wildflowers of Glacier National Park and Surrounding Areas.* Kalispell, MT: Trillium Press, 2005.

———. *Trees and Flowering Shrubs of Glacier National Park and Surrounding Areas*, 3rd ed. Kalispell, MT: Trillium Press, 2015.

Miller, O. K., and H. H. Miller. *North American Mushrooms: A Field Guide to Edible and Inedible Fungi*, Guilford, CT: FalconGuides, 2006.

Milne, L., and M. Milne. *National Audubon Society Field Guide to North American Insects & Spiders.* New York: Chanticleer Press, Inc., 2014.

Peterson, R. T. *Peterson Field Guide to Birds of Western North America*, 4th ed. Boston, MA: Houghton Mifflin Harcourt, 2010.

Phillips, H. W. *Northern Rocky Mountain Wildflowers.* Guilford, CT: FalconGuides, 2001.

———. *Central Rocky Mountain Wildflowers*, 2nd ed. Guilford, CT: FalconGuides, 2012.

Raup, O. B., R. L. Earhart, J. W. Whipple, and P. E. Carrara. *Geology Along Going-to-the-Sun Road*, 2nd ed. Tucson, AZ: Rio Nuevo Publishers, 2018.

Werner, J. K., B. A. Maxwell, P. Hendricks, and D. L. Flath. *Amphibians and Reptiles of Montana.* Missoula, MT: Mountain Press Publishing Company, 2004.

Wheeler, B. *Birds of Prey of the West.* Princeton, NJ: Princeton University Press, 2018.

Glossary

accipiter: Smaller, narrow-tailed hawks notable for their short, quick wingbeats followed by a glide.

alpine: Upper altitudes of mountain terrain where only flowers grow.

antheridia: Male part of algae, mosses, ferns, and fungi.

apothecia: Disc-like or cup-shaped fungal spores.

arthropod: Invertebrates such as crustaceans, insects, centipedes, and spiders in the phylum Euarthropoda.

banner: Single flower with two lobes typically part of a pea (legume) flower.

basal leaf: The leaves that grow toward the bottom of the stem.

bract: Modified leaves that are part of the flower head.

buteo: Larger hawks with broad wings and deep wingbeats.

cache: A hidden store of food.

cambium: A growth layer within a tree's trunk, branches, and roots.

carnivore: A meat-eating animal.

carrion: A dead, and usually rotting, animal.

cerci: Paired sensory appendages that look like pincers found at the end of some insects.

chlorophyll: The green pigment in plants, algae, and cyanobacteria that converts sunlight into energy during photosynthesis.

chrysalis: The transformation period for a butterfly from a larva to an adult.

cocoon: The silky encasement spun by some insects transforming from larval to adult stage.

conifer: An evergreen tree with needlelike leaves that bears cones.

cross-pollinated: When one plant pollinates another.

deciduous: A tree or shrub that sheds its leaves each season.

diatom: Single-celled algae with silica in the cell walls.

dioecious: A plant with either male or female flowers, requiring a corresponding plant of the opposite sex to pollinate.

elaiosome: Fleshy, usually fatty, structure on some seeds to encourage insect dispersal.

fry: Young fish within their first few months after hatching.

hemiparasitic: A plant with the ability to photosynthesize, yet taps into the roots of another plant for additional nutrients.

herbaceous: An annual, perennial, or biennial plant without a persistent woody stem.

herbivore: A plant-eating animal.

hermaphrodite: An animal with both female and male sexual organs.

hyperaccumulator: A plant that can absorb heavy metals from the soil through its roots.

incubation: The period of time required for eggs to develop and the young to emerge or hatch.

invertebrates: Animals that lack a backbone.

iridescent: The appearance of changing colors depending on the angle and light.

isidia: Vegetative reproductive structure of lichen.

krummholz: Gnarled, often stunted, wind-whipped trees in the higher elevations.

mandible: The lower jaw.

metamorphose: To undergo a change.

mollusk: Invertebrate such as a slug or a snail.

mycoheterotrophic: Plants that depend on fungi to fulfill part or all of their nutrient needs.

mycologist: Someone who studies fungi.

naiad: Aquatic larva of dragonfly, stonefly, or mayfly.

nectar: Sugary liquid produced by flowers.

nymph: Immature stage of many invertebrates.

omnivore: An animal that eats both plant and animal matter.

partial veil: The ring left on the stem of a mushroom from the covering that protects the gills when the fruit develops.

pectoral: The chest area.

perennial: Herbaceous plant that lives more than a couple of seasons.

petiole: Where the leaf attaches to the stem.

pheromone: A chemical secreted to trigger a response, often sexual, in an insect or animal.

photosynthesis: The process by which plants, algae, and cyanobacteria use sunlight to produce food.

piscicide: A chemical substance used to poison fish.

plumage: Birds' feathers.

pollen: The powdery substance produced by stamens or male cones containing male genetic material.

poultice: A moist concoction, often made up of plant materials, placed on an area for healing.

proboscis: The specialized mouthparts of some insects that allow them to extract juices from plants.

raptor: A bird of prey, such as an owl, hawk or eagle.

rhizoid: A filament often found on the bottom of mosses that anchors them to the ground.

rhizome: Perpendicularly growing fleshy stems that send out roots and shoots.

riparian: The area alongside rivers, streams, lakes, or wetlands.

saponin: A chemical in plants that causes a foaming characteristic.

serotinous: In conifers, a type of cone covered in a resin requiring fire to open it.

soredia: A group of fungal and algal cells.

sori: Clusters of spores on ferns.

spawn: When fish deposit their eggs.

spore: A stand-alone reproductive cell as part of asexual reproduction.

subalpine: The part of mountainous regions just below the tree line.

taproot: A large, dominant root typically growing directly downward.

tendrils: Stringlike, leafless parts of a plant that curl and wind themselves around structures to support the plant.

ungulate: A hoofed mammal such as elk, deer, bighorn sheep, mountain goats, and moose.

zooplankton: Sometimes, but not always, microscopic animals that move within the water column.

Index

Index

About the Author

As a media professional for over thirty years, Amy Grisak shares her passion for the outdoors through her writing, radio, podcasts, and video projects. Her career began with her decade-long work as everything from bait to associate producer for National Geographic Television, where many of the assignments involved looking for grizzlies and mountain lions instead of avoiding them. While working with these apex predators was exhilarating and educational, Amy still geeks out over nearly every flower, bird, and butterfly, and don't even get her started on pika.

Amy eventually transitioned from television to freelance writing, pairing her nature photography and field experience with her informational articles and essays in publications such as *The Farmers' Almanac, Sky & Telescope, Montana Quarterly, Distinctly Montana, The New Pioneer*, and many others. Amy is also the co-host of *Front Range Outdoors* on KGPR-Great Falls, where she and her radio partner, Marty Bannon, discuss the abundance of outdoor recreational opportunities throughout Montana.

Since the outdoors is as much a part of her daily life as it is of her work, Amy and her outdoor-loving husband, Grant, frequently take their sons, Samuel and John, hiking, fishing, and exploring their grand Montana backyard. Amy also takes particular delight talking her friends and their kids into accompanying her on hikes throughout Glacier. From a three-mile jaunt around the beaver ponds in St. Mary to the nearly ten-mile hike to Iceberg Lake with a string of kids, every outing is an adventure. Lately, as her own boys are strong enough for the bigger hikes, higher elevations beckon in search of alpine flowers, fire lookout stories, and of course those fascinating pika. Her work is found on amygrisak .com.